# The Cultural Life of Modern America

# The Cultural Life of Modern America

## by Knut Hamsun

Edited and translated by
### Barbara Gordon Morgridge

Harvard University Press
Cambridge, Massachusetts
1969

Translated from the original Norwegian edition,
*Fra det moderne Amerikas Aandsliv* (Copenhagen, 1889)

Distributed in Great Britain by Oxford University Press, London

Library of Congress Catalog Card Number 76-89970

SBN 674-17975-7

Printed in the United States of America

# Editor's Preface

With minor modification, the present translation is a literal rendering of the original Copenhagen edition of *Fra det moderne Amerikas Aandsliv* published in 1889. (For a detailed discussion of the treatment of the text, see the prefatory comment to the editor's notes.) When A. Cammermeyer became Hamsun's publisher in 1898, the firm purchased from Det Nordiske Forlag (Philipsen) the remaining copies of seven Hamsun works, including *Aandsliv*. These books were given a new title page showing the Oslo publisher and then sold to subscribers either separately or together with Cammermeyer's own editions of *Victoria* and *Sult* under the title *Skrifter*, which were issued in seventy installments.

The completion of this book is above all a tribute to friends and colleagues, to all of whom I gratefully acknowledge my dependence. I am immeasurably indebted to Einar Haugen of Harvard University, both for his patient encouragement throughout the stages of its preparation as well as for the unfailing guidance of his knowledge and scholarship. The errors that remain in meaning and interpretation are, needless to say, my own. My gratitude is also due Miss Mary MacDonald, chief of the Research and Reference Section of the Illinois State Library; the librarians of Everett Community College for their help with research materials; and the American-Scandinavian Foundation, whose fellowship provided me with an opportunity to study in Oslo, during the summer of 1966. In conclusion, I wish to thank my longtime friend and teacher, Sverre Arestad of the University of Washington, whose exhilarating dedication to Norwegian literature and unself-serving commitment to teaching and the student were at once the inspiration of my graduate studies and the seminal impulse for my interest in Knut Hamsun.

B. G. M.

*Edmonds, Washington*
*March 1969*

# Contents

# Editor's Introduction

When in 1885 the twenty-six-year-old Knut Hamsun declared the author of *The Innocents Abroad* an ill-qualified critic of European political institutions and cultural attainment, he was basing his judgment on the defects of sensitivity and perception that sprang from Twain's naively nationalistic insularity, his aesthetic ignorance, and his undeveloped, democratic view of life. Not, Hamsun readily conceded, that the account of the five-month pleasure trip through the Mediterranean to the Holy Land was uninspired or less entertaining than Twain's other books: his observations were in fact "full of humor and caprice, of clever whims and brilliant paradoxes."[1] Nevertheless, as he also pointed out, the role of successful continental critic required qualifications other than Twain's energy and natural healthy instincts. But who, the uninitiated reader may well ask, was Knut Hamsun? And what was the nature of his expectations, his personal outlook, and experience when four years later he undertook a broad and self-confident assessment of the cultural performance of late nineteenth-century America and the values, national characteristics, customs, and institutions that undergirded the nation's so-called achievements?

The "Mark Twain" essay itself was published during the brief interval between Hamsun's two sojourns in the United States; the

[1] "Mark Twain," *Ny Illustreret Tidende*, April 5, 1885, p. 110. All transtions in the introduction are by the editor.

first lasted from the beginning of 1882 until late 1884, the second from September 1886 to June 1888. Although the detailed record of these years prior to Hamsun's literary breakthrough in the 1890s has been the subject of some controversy, notably between Hamsun and his unsolicited but persistent biographer Rasmus B. Anderson, the outline of events is reasonably clear. Their beginning was in league with the times. During his unsuccessful effort to advance a literary career, Hamsun had already pursued an unstable livelihood as postal clerk and tutor, itinerant peddler, and road construction worker before he joined the large national migration to America to aid his personal fortunes. This exodus, initiated in 1825 by a small band of religious dissidents from Stavanger, had later burgeoned into the tens of thousands, until in the peak years of 1881–1885 the rate was second only to Ireland's in the percentage of total population and by 1915 totaled 754,561 emigrants—a figure in excess of four fifths of the national census of 1801.[2] Most of these emigrants were cotters and day laborers, displaced and dispossessed by Norway's transformation from an agrarian society to a modern industrial state; in external circumstance they were not unlike Hamsun himself, who was a poor farm youth from the northern province of Nordland.

But if the majority of emigrants were poor and inarticulate, although their America letters had an enormous impact on their families and friends at home, there were a number of prominent Norwegians, educated, influential, and able to reach a wider audience, who also came to the United States in these years. Some, like the Unitarian minister Kristofer Janson, were impelled by religious convictions; others, like Bjørnstjerne Bjørnson, came briefly in search of first-hand observation and knowledge. One, the noted violinist Ole Bull, had even attempted in the 1850s to establish a Norwegian colony in Pennsylvania. The most widely attended, however, was Bjørnson—poet, dramatist, novelist, and passionate de-

[2] For a comprehensive treatment of Norwegian population and immigration statistics, see Theodore C. Blegen, *Norwegian Migration to America, 1825–1860* (Northfield, Minnesota: The Norwegian-American Historical Association, 1931), pp. 4–23.

fender of the democratic cause of nineteenth-century Norwegian liberalism, who spent eight months in America in late 1880–81. His interest had been fostered in part by his republican sympathies, his extensive interest in improved economic, political, and educational opportunities for the Norwegian cotter as well as his belief in parliamentary government. He also had close personal contact with Janson, who was a sometime neighbor; Rasmus Anderson; and Ole Bull, whose American widow, Sara Thorp Bull, invited him to visit the Thorp home in Massachusetts. Here Bjørnson was introduced to the leading academic and literary figures in and about Cambridge, Longfellow, Whittier, and Emerson among them, before undertaking a strenuous and widely publicized lecture tour through the midwestern Norwegian settlements from Chicago to Fargo, North Dakota. Throughout these travels, his experiences and often enthusiastic observations and impressions were circulated in diary letters to the Norwegian Liberal press—a factor not irrelevant to Hamsun's subsequent views on American life and letters.

Hamsun's contact with Bjørnson, however, was somewhat more direct. In 1879 he had solicited Bjørnson's literary judgment in regard to his peasant tale "Frida," after failing to interest the Danish publishing house Gyldendal in its publication. Bjørnson was a recognized master of the genre, his own early literary success in the 1850s having risen from the wide popularity of such tales as "Arne" and "En Glad Gut" (A Happy Boy); yet he too could offer no encouragement, only a letter of introduction to an Oslo actor with the fruitless suggestion that the tall, handsome youth seek a career on the stage. Nevertheless, when Hamsun arrived in Madison, Wisconsin, in February 1882 he again had Bjørnson's friendly endorsement and a letter of recommendation to Rasmus Anderson, then professor of Scandinavian at the University of Wisconsin. Apparently this introduction proved unproductive; in any event, whatever Hamsun's personal expectations, his early employment was that of farmhand and, later, store clerk in or around Elroy, Wisconsin, where his brother had previously settled as a tailor. Almost immediately he also began lecturing to local Scandinavian groups on social and literary topics—among others, Bjørnson.

Somewhat later, probably in the winter or spring of 1884, Kristofer Janson discovered the young immigrant working in a lumberyard in Madelia, Minnesota, and immediately engaged him as secretary for his church. This turn of luck now introduced Hamsun to an intellectual milieu more nearly commensurate with his literary interests and aspirations, and it was here that on two occasions he sought to establish a literary foothold among his countrymen.

At the time of Hamsun's arrival in the Middle West, the cultural center of the Norwegian immigrant community had already shifted from the Wisconsin settlements to Minneapolis, where Janson had his primary pastorate. Here as elsewhere the dominant intellectual force was the Norwegian Lutheran Church, which held power both in the pulpit and in the church-sponsored press. During his lecture tour in 1881 Bjørnson had collided with this formidable and influential adversary, itself bitterly divided by controversies over means of salvation and preservation of the faith in America, because of his public renunciation of Christian dogma. But since Bjørnson was no less fervently dedicated to the cause of spiritual liberation from what he considered the tyranny of dogma, his response to clerical interference and fierce personal attack had been a spirited lecture on the fallacies of the Old Testament prophets, modern biblical criticism, theology, and the clergy. As such, the lecture reflected rationalistic currents, then strongly operative in Norway, whose elements of belief and disbelief Bjørnson with missionary zeal sought to transplant to the isolated prairies of the Midwest in an effort to loosen the hold of the Norwegian Lutheran Church. It soon became evident, however, that he had seriously miscalculated the intellectual sophistication and receptiveness of his countrymen.

Janson's twelve-year ministry in Minnesota was similarly marked and ultimately frustrated by this opposition. Although Janson had graduated with a theology degree from the University of Christiania (Oslo) in 1865, he almost simultaneously published a series of peasant tales, *Fraa Bygdom* (From the Countryside), which soon won him considerable popularity. Then in 1869 he accepted a private teaching position and for the next nine years devoted himself to Christopher Bruun's folk high school in Gudbrandsdalen—an outgrowth of the educational movement originated by N.F.S. Grundtvig in Denmark and designed to raise the intellectual level and political consciousness of the rural population. At the same time, through his intimate association with Bjørnson in these years, he had come under the sway of rationalistic thought, and his gradual defection from orthodox belief led at the close of the 1870s to his dismissal from the school post. By now a poet and writer of some note, he soon decided to make a lecture tour through the Norwegian settlements of the United States. Here, like Bjørnson a year later, he was impressed by the material improvement and independence of the former Norwegian cotters; but he noted the pervasive ignorance of these people and was particularly critical of the cultural indifference and uncouth behavior of the first-generation youth, for which he blamed their parents and the Norwegian Lutheran Church.

The impetus for this visit, which Janson described in his published impressions of the United States, issued from his profound and moving response to Walt Whitman's *Democratic Vistas,* then recently translated into Danish by Rudolf Schmidt. "I recommend it," he wrote in *Amerikanske Forholde, Fem Foredrag* (American Conditions, Five Lectures), "to all those who wish to read something beautiful, manly, enthusiastic, and timely. Rarely have I read a nobler and more remarkable book. It was this book that especially drew me to America and that allows me to hope in America as the land of the future—and to do so in spite of the fact that there is no one who, in their unadorned nakedness, has called attention to the blemishes in American society as has he."[3] One consequence of Janson's tour was the collection of lectures which both in format and general subject matter foreshadow Hamsun's own book at the end of the decade. A second altered his future more radically. Before leaving the United States in 1880, Janson has become acquainted with the liberal religious writings of William Ellery Channing, Theodore Parker, and James Freeman Clarke; thus when Rasmus

[3] Copenhagen, 1881, p. 76.

Anderson wrote to him the following year asking him to assume leadership of a free religious movement based in Minneapolis and supported by the Unitarians, Janson accepted.

During the twelve-year pastorate that ensued, Janson rapidly distinguished himself as an enlightened figure among his countrymen: in his undogmatic spiritual ministry, in his championing of social reform, and in his unflagging dedication to a deeper intellectual awareness that sought to preserve contact with Norwegian arts and letters. Already a prolific writer in fields both secular and religious, he now became a popular lecturer; he contributed actively to the Norwegian-American press, particularly the liberal and progressive weekly *Budstikken;* and with his talented wife, Drude, Janson made his home available for weekly literary discussion groups, with lively exchanges of ideas as well as music and song that quickly attracted the intellectuals of the Scandinavian community. Yet the obstacles that Bjørnson had encountered during his tour remained to hamper and ultimately to terminate Janson's efforts to transform the cultural environment of the Norwegian church-centered immigrants.

Although Janson's activities received favorable notice in the Norwegian papers at home, perhaps the most informative evaluation of his literary merits and cultural accomplishments in the Scandinavian Northwest emerges from Hamsun's essay "Kristofer Janson," which was published in the Danish journal *Ny Jord* in October 1888. Noteworthy, too, as an early statement of his own aesthetic criteria, Hamsun's analysis is at once incisive and sensitive, even gentle, particularly in the light of his admitted inability to appreciate the moral, pedagogical, and religious qualities of his former employer. This bias notwithstanding, the essay ungrudgingly acknowledges Janson as "one of literature's delegates," because of his inherent lyric and narrative powers; at the same time, however, it denies him more than secondary literary rank. That Janson did fall short of his creative promise, that his writings failed to achieve the status of genuine art, resulted from conscious choice, since he was unwilling to subordinate his life's work, that of popular educator of his countrymen, to the rigorous demands of art. As Janson himself admitted, he did not aspire to please the aestheticians. Rather, his literary works—in their

human insights, in their diction, in their informing moral purpose—
were consciously controlled to meet popular needs and an average
level of understanding. Nor was it only the limitations of Janson's
didacticism and the extraordinary demands on his mind and energy
which undercut his cultural leadership in Minneapolis. Although
the role had been forced upon him by his very prominence, he
lacked, in Hamsun's opinion, both the aggressiveness and the intellectual precision to make a really forceful, creative leader—a criticism, doubtless, that discloses something of the motive for Hamsun's
permanent return to Scandinavia in 1888. Significantly, the concluding image of Janson, with its attendant implication of cultural
barrenness, is that of "the noblest public figure we have of Norwegians in the West—a solitary, delicate flower on a North American prairie."[4]

It was in this environment, under Janson's leadership, that Hamsun now found himself, and with his zest for living, his conviviality,
and his originality he proved a notable asset. But if his new secre-
tarial duties gave him an opportunity to unfold his creative and
forensic talents as well as the leisure to read and wrestle with his
style, this more comfortable respite in the Janson home was short-
lived and ended abruptly. In the autumn of 1884 he fell seriously
ill, his condition diagnosed as tuberculosis, and when faced with a
fatal prognosis he was determined to return home as soon as possible.

Here the record grows somewhat uncertain. Nevertheless, despite
the urgency of Hamsun's departure, other evidence suggests that he
was sufficiently recovered on the first leg of his journey to "travel
about some" in the East. In the Twain essay Hamsun remarks in
passing that he had once talked with the humorist. Twain had
entered semi-retirement from the lecture circuits after his marriage
in 1870, and although he subsequently lectured in England and
appeared frequently as an after-dinner speaker in the United States,
it was not until late 1884 that he again took to the road with George
Cable. Their tour opened in New Haven on November 5, and by
Christmas of that year they had played several eastern cities before

---

[4] "Kristofer Janson," p. 386.

starting a long series of engagements in the Middle West. It was probably in mid-November, then, while Twain was appearing in New York and Brooklyn, that Hamsun had an opportunity to see a performance and speak with Twain personally.[5] That Hamsun spent some time in the East prior to leaving the United States is supported further by the fact that his three-part article "Fra Amerika" (From America), which appeared in early 1885, includes a number of impressions of New York.

Back in Norway, Hamsun had an opportunity to regain his health, working as a postal clerk and attempting to forward his literary interests by lectures and occasional contributions to Norwegian journals and newspapers. Then, in the late winter of 1886, he went to Oslo to write, an experience of defiant self-preservation that later provided a wealth of material for his first novel, *Hunger*. But, as Janson observed of Hamsun's renewed efforts to establish himself in Norway, "he could not do without *food*, and for the second time he fled across the Atlantic."[6] The purpose of his return was apparently largely financial: he was deeply in debt and unable to meet his obligations in Norway. By late September he was in Chicago doing manual labor for a railroad, with a promising future, so he wrote, as a cable-car conductor. Yet this promising employment probably lasted little more than a few months. Nor does his poverty seem to have been greatly assuaged, according to what fragmentary information we have. The first certain knowledge of his activities in 1887 appears in *Budstikken,* indicating that by April he was involved once more in the parochial cultural affairs of the Scandinavian community in Minneapolis, preparing to lecture on Kristofer Janson at Dania Hall. The following month he contributed a letter defending a public reading of Christian Krohg's *Albertine,* which in Norway had been confiscated as pornographic on December 20, 1886, the day after its publication.

Although Hamsun eventually sought summer employment with

<hr>

[5] Paul Fatout, *Mark Twain on the Lecture Circuit* (Bloomington: Indiana University Press, 1960), pp. 204–231.

[6] *Hvad jeg har oplevet, livserindringer* (Kristiania: Gyldendalske Boghandel Nordisk Forlag, 1913), p. 221.

a farm crew on the Oliver Dalrymple farm, an immense wheat operation in the Red River Valley, he returned to Minneapolis with the
intention of maintaining himself on his summer earnings and what
proved to be a very meager income from a projected lecture series.
Many years later Krøger Johansen, who also describes Hamsun's
intense drive to create a distinctive, original style during this period,
related that he had met Hamsun that fall at a social gathering at
Janson's church and Hamsun had detailed a plan. "He now felt,"
Johansen recalled in a *Dagbladet* article on January 18, 1903,[7]
"—and he swore mildly—that he understood literature better than
any person in Minnesota. It was his métier, so to speak, and he
genuinely believed that he possessed indisputable talent in that
respect." If he could but gather some publicity from the least bigoted
of the local papers and if Janson would announce his project from
the pulpit, he was convinced that he could earn enough to keep himself in tobacco throughout the winter as well as buy a pair of badly
needed galoshes.

This plan for a series of Sunday afternoon talks, eleven in all
during the winter of 1887–88, was realized and apparently made
Hamsun something of a local celebrity, according to the later recol-
lections of his friends (many of whom became prominent journalists
in Minneapolis). The content of this series is briefly sketched in the
Swedish-language paper *Svenska Folkets Tidning* and reflects Hamsun's interest in modern currents of world literature, beginning with
the French naturalists and ranging through such contemporary
Scandinavian writers as Ibsen, Bjørnson, Janson, Alexander Kielland, Jonas Lie, and Strindberg. Two of these lecture topics were
also related to later essays: one, entitled "August Strindberg," he sold
to the American journal *America* the following summer; the second
was his critical evaluation of Janson.

A final notice in *Svenska Folkets Tidning* bears directly upon the
accelerated tempo of Hamsun's development in 1888, after a winter
of intense literary activity. In April he presented a lecture to a
Scandinavian-American audience at Dania Hall entitled "Sociale og

---

[7] Under the pseudonym Cecil Krøger.

æstetiske Tanker—Livet i Minneapolis" (Social and Aesthetic Observations: Life in Minneapolis). Although the lecture as such is not preserved, a subsequent April 25 item on Kristofer Janson casts some light on its content. Janson, it appears, had felt compelled to answer with a second lecture on the same topic, consisting in part of a refutation of Hamsun's assessment, his principal argument being that on the whole Hamsun had "employed too large a yardstick for our young city." A second feature of the lecture, a humorous description of an evening at an Italian folk theater, was conceived as "a companion piece to the usual productions of the People's Theater, which Hamsun censured so sharply." This brief comment not only establishes a direct link between the repeated comparisons with Minneapolis in Hamsun's *Cultural Life;* it also serves to illustrate the inflation of personal experience that underlies many of the generalizations in his subsequent study of America. When these criticisms reappear there, they denote general characteristics of the American theater public and players; but the immediate inspiration for Hamsun's comments on their uncouth behavior and low level of artistic discernment was apparently the People's Theater in Minneapolis, which during the week of Janson's lecture, for example, was performing *The Streets of New York,* with admission prices of 10, 20, and 30 cents. Other materials in *Cultural Life,* such as the sentiments issuing from the Chicago Haymarket riot and the eventual execution of four anarchists, are similarly tied to Hamsun's personal involvement in the topical affairs of Minneapolis and the social, cultural, and political interests that shaped the intellectual profile of that limited Scandinavian-American milieu. It was also the limitations and dissatisfactions of this milieu, implicit in *Cultural Life,* together with the mounting pressures from his artistic talent, that determined his resolve to leave the United States in the early summer of 1888.

When in mid-July the *Thingvalla* docked at Copenhagen with Hamsun aboard, he immediately settled in a garret in the working quarter and began to write. As so often in the rootless years of literary apprenticeship, he was extremely poor, and the outline of his renewed contest with physical deprivation, nervous exhaustion, and the insatiable urgings of artistic expression is poignantly, even pathetically, limned in his letters for the remainder of the year. It is from this painful matrix of physical hardship, desperation, and tenacious endurance that his first novel eventually issued—a study, as he described it, "of the nuances of hunger, a starving person's shifting states of mind."[8] Before its completion and against his will, although his identity was temporarily concealed, he was forced to submit a portion of it for publication; but while it earned him a desperately needed advance from Philipsen's Publishing House and offers from two publishers for future works, he had become so physically and emotionally depleted that he was temporarily unable to finish the book. Finally in early December, despite an occasional newspaper article and the publication of the *Hunger* fragment and his essay on Janson, he was reduced to soliciting financial help from an Oslo merchant, Johan Sørensen, whose aid fortunately was immediately forthcoming.

It was thus Sørensen who received a progress report on another piece of writing, now nearing completion. Its topic was the cultural life of America, and it would, the author confidently announced, strongly oppose "the grand notions of America in the Scandinavian press."[9] Furthermore, Hamsun had found an audience in the Student Association at the University of Copenhagen, which he addressed twice, first in December and again in January. Originally he had been asked to speak on the American political economist and sociologist, Henry George, but had suggested instead that he discuss his impressions of the United States with the understanding that he be given free rein since, as he emphasized in advance, his views "on the majority of points deviated from the usual, among others, also from Bjørnson's."[10] His reception, however, was enthusiastic and unreserved. He was no less gratified by the reaction of the Danish publisher Philipsen, who approached him immediately after the

[8] Tore Hamsun, *Knut Hamsun som han var, et utvalg av hans brev* (Oslo: Gyldendal Norsk Forlag, 1956), p. 41. Quoted by permission of Tore Hamsun.

[9] *Ibid.*, p. 43.

[10] *Ibid.*, p. 48.

first lecture with the succinct announcement that he would publish the lectures. There was as well the exhilaration of warm public approval from the dean of Danish critics, Georg Brandes, who rose at the close of the second lecture to speak in his behalf.

Still, the renewed struggle against literary anonymity was not yet won, as Hamsun's increasingly vigorous stratagems to awaken critical interest and attention readily attest—efforts, moreover, that suggest that his immediate artistic intention with *Cultural Life* was less genuine social criticism than calculated self-advertisement. In the letter to Sørensen, Hamsun had underscored the disparity between his views and those current in Scandinavia, and for a time he even imagined that this might jeopardize Philipsen's acceptance of his lectures. But by March, with publication assured, he was predicting that his independent outlook was certain to arouse heated contention in both the Liberal and Conservative press, with perhaps Bjørnson leading the attack. He was in fact so convinced of the radical and controversial content of his book that in a March 4 letter to the Swedish-American critic in Minneapolis, Victor Nilsson, he foresaw the possibility of confiscation, the far-reaching publicity effects of which he had witnessed earlier in connection with Krohg's *Albertine*. The letter also contains some more intimate disclosures about the composition and intention of his book, an expanded and revised version of his lectures: "It is so absolutely subjective all the way through, and during its preparation I've had no works to refer to— just my memory and a number of notations scattered about in lectures and notebooks. But I think the book is tolerably interesting, for it is different from other books on America, asserts *my* lopsided view of the land of the Philistines and is violently oppositional. Here at home all the newspapers will be downright abusive toward me because of it—in fact, it may be confiscated. So I'll gain no laurels for it. But if I can succeed in getting it through people's heads that I have literary power, despite my lopsided view, then I'll be satisfied nevertheless."[11]

If the subordination of social conviction to literary talent is implied

[11] *Ibid.*, pp. 59–60.

in Hamsun's candid admission to Nilsson, what has been called his grasp of American advertising techniques is evident in other correspondence, in which he persistently and unabashedly seeks public acknowledgment from established writers and critics in both Scandinavia and America. In April 1889, for example, he again turned to Nilsson, not only requesting notice of his forthcoming book in *Svenska Folkets Tidning* but seeking Nilsson's influence in persuading the noted Swedish writer Gustaf af Geijerstam to do a review for the Swedish papers. In turn he could report that Brandes was submitting a critique, which appeared in *Verdens Gang* on May 9, 1889, and he anticipated that the Danish critic would discuss the book's literary merit and philosophy of life. He added that "the only man here at home, besides Georg Brandes, who will defend my book's radical opinions is *Arne Garborg* in Norway."[12]

In actuality, this estimate of his controversiality and radicalism as well as of his critics proved largely a construct of Hamsun's overeager imagination. Bjørnson remained silent, and so did Garborg. And though Brandes praised the author as a "new and outstanding" prose writer, his comments, instead of defending Hamsun's outlook, focused upon its temperamental and environmental origins. Nor could he, in commending the stylistic excellence of the book, completely resist the temptation "to tease a teaser and pull the seat out from under one who has seated himself on the mockers' bench." Other notices in the Scandinavian press were few in number, but none was hostile. When the ardent liberal, Kristofer Kristoferson, wrote in *Dagbladet* on April 26, 1889, he called the book the most devastating judgment of American conditions to reach Norway, presented "in an artistic form which is rare even in older writers of distinction." With the accuracy of the judgments he refused to take issue. Like Brandes, however, he isolated Hamsun's stylistic indebtedness to American examples: "Well, he finds little to praise in the Yankee, but there is nevertheless one thing—and by no means a bad one—that Hamsun himself has learned from him. It is his delivery. Not a man in the world can talk as long about one topic

[12] *Ibid.*, p. 97.

to an audience that does not get bored as the Yankee can. No one is so full of unexpected whims in the midst of seriousness; no one can come so seductively with a dry jest, a single word, that for an instant sweeps away into a cascade of merriment; absolutely no one can be so richly varied in style. And it is from him he has learned it, this Yankee-chastizer Hamsun. He has learned to entertain while he preaches."

Although Edvard Brandes also submitted a review, the most important attention still came from Georg Brandes, who welcomed

> this extremely well-written book with which a nervous, straining more than searching talent makes his debut. There is something well-calculated to attract attention—first in the book's spirit, in its hatred of all that is coarse and gross and inartistic, even if it is called popular, free, and moral—thereafter in the book's form which, despite the author's unceasing attack on everything American because of his unconscious, nervous impressionability toward his surroundings, has become completely American—disjointed, cutting, humorously exaggerated, striving after effect and, as a rule, achieving the effect.

With its tempo and hilarity, this unadulterated American style was admirably suited to the book's purpose—"an energetic protest and satire"—whose origins lay in Hamsun's aristocratic nature. At the same time, Brandes emphasized the distinction between the book's unusual merit in style and technique and the nature of its perceptions; and as Hamsun had criticized Emerson for lacking the sympathy and psychological penetration necessary for true critical understanding, so he too, in his interpretations of American society and culture, was partly vulnerable to the same charge. It was a distinction, moreover, that belied Hamsun's confident prediction to Nilsson that Brandes, especially, would support his radicalism. "With him as a guide," Brandes wrote, "we do not get down to the sources of life in that great land. Here is jeering done with extraordinary talent but less understanding. There is not a country in the world, the reader feels, about which one could not write a similar satire." "What a burlesque," he wryly added, "could be written about 'the cultural life' of the three Scandinavian countries!"

When somewhat later Kristofer Janson published his lengthy review of *Cultural Life* on the other side of the Atlantic, it conformed on the whole with Brandes' aesthetic estimate. But whereas Scandinavian critics had registered the subjectivity in Hamsun's commentary, their reactions tended to be general because their perspective was largely European. Janson, on the other hand, spoke from an intimate, first-hand knowledge of the immigrant milieu that had shaped the background for Hamsun's judgments. For in spite of the fact that the book assigned its criticisms to America at large and commented authoritatively on middle-class society and various social phenomena, it is apparent in the frequent illustrations from Minneapolis and the Dakota prairies that Hamsun's impressions were garnered from this rude, transitional environment, with its farmers and workingmen, rather than from any intimate contact with the educated classes in the longer-established areas of the eastern United States. Accordingly, Janson's review often took issue with the exaggerations and inaccuracies in Hamsun's personal documentation, and he repeated in part his earlier reply to Hamsun's lecture on life in Minneapolis. Moreover, because of Janson's religious convictions, democratic sympathies, and temperamental incompatibility with his subject, at once aesthetic and perhaps personal, he was openly critical of what Brandes had only sought to define in the Norwegian's basic response to experience. Not only did Janson consider the aristocratic demand for an intellectual elite as "infinitely old-fashioned, medieval"; he charged that it was inconsistent with Hamsun's claim to intellectual modernity. It sprang, he maintained, from his "sickly longing for a coterie dedicated to beauty, surrounded by a little world of its own making which can exclude all that is offensive to one's craving for beauty."[13] This attitude, the more remarkable because of the seemingly inhospitable circumstances of Hamsun's birth and development, was both the source of the writer's onesidedness and the book's weakness. Yet

[13] Janson's "Knut Hamsuns Bog om Amerika" appeared in *Budstikken* June 26, July 3, 10, 17, 1889; the quotation is from the final installment.

despite such reservations Janson joined in hailing Hamsun's debut and the "fine stylistic talent" it betokened. The four long installments of his review ran in *Budstikken* during the summer of 1889, marking the last extended public discussion of the book.

Although the preceding survey provides a perspective for the immediate literary and personal context of *Cultural Life's* publication, it is a perspective that temporarily frustrates the reader's understanding of Hamsun's attitudes toward America. In calling the study "an energetic protest and satire," Brandes had raised the issue of the relation between tone and treatment, on the one hand, and conviction, on the other—an estimate complicated by the self-dramatizing and self-advertising strain in Hamsun's insistent claim to an independent, highly individualized outlook. The intended reliability of his presentation is further complicated by the pervasive evidence of suppression, manipulation, and outright fabrication that has now been uncovered in his documentary materials and detailed in the annotation of this translation. Finally, there is the author's own repudiation of this "youthful sin" and his inflexible refusal to allow republication of the book. The history of this refusal, not without its own element of ambiguity, is briefly sketched in his answer to his publisher, Harald Grieg, who in connection with Gyldendal's fiftieth-anniversary edition of Hamsun's collected works sought permission in 1939 to include *Cultural Life*. "It is much too inferior a book," the eighty-year-old author replied. "Strindberg wrote that I had seen America more clearly than he and others (in a letter to Brandes), but I myself got tired of the book. When an American publishing house wanted to translate it, I said no. When Kønig wanted to reprint it, I was again heroically firm of character, and I'll just say to you now that if you should ever get hold of a copy of this book, quietly lay it on that large heap of my other sins."[14] What, then, is the larger perspective from which to consider the book?

To begin with, although *Cultural Life* presents the most sustained

[14] *Fra det moderne Amerikas Aandsliv*, introd. Tore Hamsun (Oslo: Gyldendal Norsk Forlag, 1962), p. xxii. Quoted by permission of Tore Hamsun.

treatment of its subject, it is neither the exclusive nor the exhaustive source of insight into its author's views. In addition to varied newspaper polemics, scattered autobiographical comment, and the more oblique testimony of Hamsun's short stories and novels, there are two closely related discussions that precede its composition and two others that at greater intervals follow it. The "Mark Twain" essay appeared in March-April 1885, and recently Harald Næss has identified another Hamsun article, "Fra Amerika," under the signature "Ego" in *Aftenposten's* files for January 21 and February 12 and 14, 1885. Then in 1908 Hamsun revived the topic in an open letter to the Danish writer Johannes V. Jensen and again two decades later in an article entitled "What Is Progress?" which was requested by the *St. Louis Post-Dispatch.* Together they span a period of more than forty years and record the changing outlook that begins with the ambitious literary aspirant, intent upon artistic recognition, and ends with the internationally acknowledged Nobel Prize winner who successfully eluded a delegation of prominent well-wishers on the occasion of his seventieth birthday in 1929.

In anticipation of the Copenhagen lectures, "Mark Twain" advances the fundamental premise that the conditions of American life and temperament are largely incompatible with the realization of distinctly national and representative art forms, in part because the creative energies of the nation are almost exclusively invested in material interests and the pursuit of power and social influence, in part because the overriding demand for patriotic conformity to these goals is basically inimical to individual genius and original self-expression. With a single exception, the harvest of significant literature is thus both meager and imitative, with even its more talented practitioners having failed to liberate themselves from English tradition. The exception is American humor, at once a native genre of considerable intellectual power and individuality and the most distinctive element in the country's cultural life. Its popular success had its roots in the American national character, turning on the impatience of the reading public with more demanding writers as well as a national predilection for "noisy entertainment" rather than introspective analysis. Of the six humorists identified, "the greatest and most representative" is Twain, whose claim to literary distinction lay in the extraordinary vitality and comic inventiveness of his language and the variety and fidelity of his observations, especially in regard to contemporary American life. The most detailed critical scrutiny, however, is reserved for *The Innocents Abroad* and the judgments it embodies, an examination that also illustrates Hamsun's thesis that as continental critic Twain, no less than the American public in general, exhibited the larger limitations of a way of life and mode of government to which Hamsun attributes the nation's artistic mediocrity.

At the same time, the essay reveals that Hamsun had encountered, with both aesthetic appreciation and receptivity, a comic style of hyperbole, paradox, and wit which helped to shape the tone and treatment of his American experiences in *Cultural Life*. We see this also in "Fra Amerika." But there the sweep of critical interest moves from a single literary figure, more or less objectively appraised, to a broader concern with the distinguishing characteristics of the American people, particularly the New Yorker. As the pseudonym "Ego" suggests, despite its masking of identity, the vehicle of "Fra Amerika" is personal reportage, impressionistic and anecdotal in its shifting focus; yet it soberly lays claim to the reliability that issues from "personal experiences" and the exclusive use of "accurate sources." In this it anticipates the documentary scheme of *Cultural Life*. But the article is less dogmatically onesided in its survey, even if it is clearly a rehearsal of the later work both in themes and in details of content. It, too, registers the nervous, straining pace of American life and is critical of the ceaseless, all-consuming hunger not for the essentials of survival as elsewhere in the world, but for physical well-being; nevertheless, it betrays a certain ambivalent fascination with the scale, the speculative boldness, the skill and ingenuity of American enterprise, however grotesque its manifestations, which derived from the "more fortunate" aspects of the country's racial mixture. Later, these mechanical and mathematical aptitudes would be dismissed as irrelevant to the issue of culture.

Two other features stand forth when the article is contrasted with the book. First, "Fra Amerika" expresses strong personal disappointment over the disparity between idealistic expectation and the disillusionment of actual encounter, between the admirable principles of brotherhood, equality, and freedom enunciated by the Declaration of Independence and the overwhelming license permitted by the nation's free institutions. Although the extreme bias of *Cultural Life* has often been viewed as a conscious reaction to Bjørnson's enthusiasm for America, the opposition here specifically isolates Janson, whose series of published lectures in 1881 had favorably reviewed American conditions, and his contention that "as soon as one goes ashore in America one sees one is in a free country." At this stage, however, Hamsun does not seem to locate the fault in the principles of American democracy themselves but in the nation's lack of moral development—a development constantly frustrated and indeed endangered by the immigrant tides of "sick and ruined human raw materials" from Europe and elsewhere. "If the Americans of today," he wrote, "were a single people who from the start had grown thoroughly familiar with human rights and freedoms and not a mixture of the most disparate racial elements from every corner of the world, well, then America would be what we idealistically believe it to be before we go there, and then socially it would be generations ahead of nations as it now morally lies generations behind."[15] As a partial aid to national viability, one utterly untenable four years later, he proposed that immigration either be halted entirely or at least restricted.

The second important feature of "Fra Amerika" casts a revealing light on Hamsun's subsequent assessment of Walt Whitman. In a fleeting compliment to the poet in "Mark Twain," Hamsun excludes him from the common run of English imitators, and again in "Fra Amerika" he describes him as America's only "modern poet" and "a very important man" whom his countrymen refused to acknowledge because of his coarseness. But as a reading of *Cultural Life* makes clear, Hamsun's now largely negative evaluation is dictated by the necessities of his thesis and satiric mode as well as, probably, the erosion of his earlier democratic sympathies. Whitman and Emerson

[15] "Fra Amerika, I," *Aftenposten*, January 21, 1885.

alike, Hamsun indicates at the conclusion of the literary section, were not only familiar to European audiences; they had been recognized as "especially national representatives of their country's literature." Therefore, by reducing the one to "an inarticulate poet" and the other to a "literary homilist," their disparagement served to confirm both his general estimate of intellectual and artistic inferiority and his specific panacea, that of guidance and instruction from more advanced European nations whose superior cultural products were being severely hampered by the misguided patriotism of congressional tariff restrictions.

Yet however confident its assessment, the treatment in *Cultural Life* discloses no truly sustained critical effort to plumb the meaning of either writer. Nor does it survive unblemished a careful collation of original sources and translations. *Representative Men,* which Hamsun tenders as Emerson's major philosophical work, is particularly mistranslated and quoted out of context, as the notes disclose. In the Whitman analysis, the shorter and more superficial of the two, Hamsun cultivates the image of a goodhearted, sensitive, but talentless and self-absorbed primitive in order to discredit Whitman's reputation as prosodic innovator and poet of democracy, interpretations, it should be noted, previously urged in Scandinavia by Janson, Bjørnson, and the Danish critic Rudolf Schmidt. To this end and with the added device of an often feigned naiveté, he dwells on the obscurities of Whitman's language and the excesses of his catalogues in a lively commentary on unrelated passages that often disregards both context and thematic continuity. As a consequence of this comic disparagement, with its concentration on the personal and idiosyncratic, the analysis ignores the representative voice of *Leaves of Grass* and never comes to grips with the poet's aspirations for the individual and for democracy.

If the strategy with Whitman is thus broadly satiric in its reduction of his literary inventiveness and artistic significance, the subsequent handling of Emerson grants that writer larger concessions of education, stylistic distinction, and understanding, but it, too, seeks to disparage vis-à-vis European excellence. Aided in part by examples and ideas gleaned from Henry Norman's "Ralph Waldo Emerson:

An Ethical Study" in the *Fortnightly Review,* Hamsun's treatment pivots on the formula that Emerson operated as a moralist in his literary criticism and as a Unitarian in his moral philosophy. These factors account for the defects in his critical insight and philosophy. At the same time, by exploiting the characteristic overstatement in Emerson's epigramatic style and the inconsistencies of logic in his mode of transcendentalism, Hamsun evolves his own satiric mosaic of illogicality and inconsistency—a technique of incongruous juxtaposition of quotations, judicious omission and translational alteration, that effectively serves his clever, irreverent critical exploration. But once again, despite a number of critical insights, it is an analysis that both neglects Emerson's other writings, which are essential to an intelligible discussion of his philosophic outlook, as well as assiduously avoids any genuine effort to define or distinguish between Unitarianism and transcendentalism; yet the latter provides the moral and philosophic framework for Emerson's biographical inquiry into the "uses of great men," the objective of *Representative Men.* In short, Hamsun again employs a technique which, rather than seeking to base the critical assessment on understanding, manifests itself in a consistently entertaining, sometimes striking, but thoroughly disabling judgment that places the critic in prominent and flattering relief. And this perhaps is the dominant impression that emerges from the implicit comparison thus drawn between Hamsun and his American subjects—a comparison which, whatever else it may be, readily displays the wit, the boldness of judgment, and stylistic virtuosity of the critic.

Precisely these features of Hamsun's total study drew an immediate and highly favorable response from contemporary reviewers; for however he might fare with his "lopsided view," he had now impressively demonstrated to the world of Scandinavian letters that he indeed possessed "literary power." The priority of these two considerations is evidenced in his rapidly unfolding literary production and attendant intellectual concerns. After a few retaliatory thrusts at his critics—Brandes' criticism in particular having nicked a sensitive nerve—Hamsun's interest in America drops from view. He does not again mention the topic publicly until a decade and a half later, and then his comments fall within a larger commentary on Johannes V. Jensen's *Den ny Verden* (The New World), a loosely knit series of essays dealing with the theme of popular democracy, chiefly in the United States and Denmark. This broader theme is captured in the title of Hamsun's review, "Bondekulturen" (Rural Culture), which in the form of an open letter was published in the Danish literary journal *Tilskueren* in 1908. Here in response to Jensen's interpretation of contemporary American life, Hamsun pointedly denies its reliability and in a revealing comparison adds: "I know of nothing that can better be compared with your unfounded comment on society in the United States of America than my own youthful sin on the same subject from the opposite point of view; I, however, discount the fact that my treatise, as far as I remember, was so appallingly badly and childishly written."[16]

The comparison is broadly useful. Insofar as Jensen's book reacts to the temper and tempo of early twentieth-century America, it is as enthusiastically favorable as, Hamsun concedes, his own book had been onesidedly critical. From the standpoint of his own developing outlook on contemporary life, however, the more instructive parallel emerges in the juxtaposition of Hamsun's "Under halvmånen" (Under the Crescent Moon)—the personal account, appearing two years before, of his travels in Turkey at the turn of the century—and the impressionistic, kaleidoscopic sketches of American life, literature, and personalities in the early chapters of *Den ny Verden*. Despite the incompatibility of their views, there is in both a strong current of responsive approval: in Hamsun for the leisurely, pretechnological, tradition-bound life in the Near East; in Jensen for the restless, even brutal surge of American democracy. In both writings as well, critical consciousness resides less in a complex scrutiny of the new than in an opposition to certain salient features of the old world of Western civilization. Moreover, if *Den ny Verden* has its obvious referent in the New World, the title is emblematic for the democratic and technical-scientific thrust of the twentieth century in Europe and in the United States, with its roots,

---

[16] *Tilskueren*, xxv (1908), 107.

according to Jensen, in the land and the farmers. This analysis Hamsun opposes: first, in regard to the contributions of rural culture, the major focus of Jensen's argument; second, in reference to Jensen's more peripheral illustrations from America. The significance of Hamsun's disparagement of *Cultural Life* also begins to fall into perspective here. As becomes evident, his concern is largely with its rigidly biased presentation, not its essential viewpoint, since he continues to attack the restless, material strivings of the modern world, which now characterized not only American but European and even Norwegian society as well. "We are all being splendidly Americanized," he notes ironically, "and we shout with rapture."[17] America, in other words, still functions as a convenient label for his disapproval of dominant contemporary trends, but "Americanism" in its broadest reach has come to embrace developments in the entire Western world. This expansion of meaning is foreshadowed in the earlier "Under halvmånen," with its suggestion of an opposing set of values for "fools who are unable to see the world's salvation and life in the future merely in railroad construction, socialism, and American clamor."[18] And it is these values, informing Hamsun's novels of the second and third decades of this century, which link "Under halvmånen" and "Bondekulturen" with Hamsun's final extended statement on American life and culture.

The occasion arose in connection with the fiftieth anniversary edition of the *St. Louis Post-Dispatch* in 1928. The invitation came from Joseph Pulitzer, the founder's son, who explained that the paper was devoting its editorial columns to a series of appraisals of modern civilization. Although Hamsun's contribution—entitled in translation "What Is Progress?"—did not appear in the anniversary edition, it was prominently featured on the editorial page of the December 30 issue. Here, in pondering this and similar requests for "et fyndord å leve på" (a sustaining word of wisdom) which might aid the confused and godless gropings of mankind for peace and inner contentment, Hamsun establishes the basic dichotomy between

---

[17] *Ibid.*, p. 99.
[18] Knut Hamsun, *Samlede verker*, 5th ed. (Oslo: Gyldendal Norsk Forlag, 1954), IV, 311.

the ever-accelerating speed, activity, and mechanical efficiency of the contemporary Western world, especially as witnessed in the United States, and the competing ethical wisdom of the Eastern world as capsulated in the Augustinian words *festina lente*.[19] And herein lies his fundamental criticism of the technological orientation of the West: "We become civilized, overcivilized, but we lose in spirit." Genuine culture, on the contrary, has its roots in tradition and the reverence for tradition that are revealed in the contrast between American skyscrapers and the profound cultural values inherent in Trondheim's cathedral and royal residence.

At the same time, although Hamsun continues to reject American goals and ambitions, he is after forty years more generous in his estimate of the people, notably their helpfulness, sympathy, and generosity, of which he now recalls numerous instances from his own experiences. His estimate of America's cultural status has altered, too, the dark forebodings of *Cultural Life* notwithstanding, and in this he especially acknowledges the flowering of the American novel as "the freshest and most original in the world—a renewal and an example for Europe." Finally, the article pays warm tribute to the nation's respect for the dignity and importance of individual endeavor. Given a head and hands to work with, the ordinary American uses both throughout his lifetime. This is to his credit and again offers a worthy example for world emulation. Yet Hamsun's recognition of these positive features in the country's cultural life and character remains qualified by an abiding opposition to the materialistic values and ambitions of American society, in which the spiritual losses tend to vitiate accomplishment—an opposition that he had initially expressed in "Fra Amerika" and "Mark Twain" and satirically exploited in *Cultural Life*. As for the true goal of progress, it is, he concludes, peace and repose of the body and spirit, a state at once ethical, nonmaterial, and aesthetic, whose successful realization lay preserved in yet another enduring impression from his past: that of the poetry, leisurely pace, and simple contentment of the Persian

[19] Quotations are translated from the original article, "Festina Lente," *Aftenposten*, December 12, 1928.

hackdrivers he had encountered during his travels in the Near East at the turn of the century.

Against this background, the ambiguity noted in Hamsun's reply to Harald Grieg concerning the inclusion of *Cultural Life* in his collected works appears to be resolved. It is true that, from the vantage point of half a century, Hamsun described that study as "much too inferior" and enjoined his publisher to consign it to the heap of his other sins. But he also chose to recall Strindberg's statement that he, Hamsun, "had seen America more clearly than he and others," and this evaluation he did not challenge, whatever his other reservations. Thirty years earlier, on the other hand, in comparing his book with Jensen's *Den ny Verden,* he had specifically isolated the unfounded commentary in both, while admitting further that his own was poorly and childishly written. To these admissions we can add the repeated instances of superficiality and bluff, of misrepresentation, inaccuracy, and fabrication that have now been exposed in *Cultural Life's* sources and documentation but whose detailed presence earlier was known only to Hamsun. On the whole, then, this evidence of unreliability as well as Hamsun's personal estimate appear limited to the manner of his presentation and documentation. As his statement to Grieg indicates, they do not repudiate his essential view of American life and society, despite certain shifts in interest, emphasis, and memory.

Within the compass of Hamsun's total literary production, a final feature of his relationship to America becomes apparent, that is, its largely preparatory nature. *Cultural Life* in effect marks the culmination of a literary apprenticeship that looks backward to his articles of the 1880s and his lectures in Minneapolis, but not forward to his career in imaginative literature that began with *Hunger* in 1890. For a time Hamsun did defend the validity of his assessment in *Cultural Life,* but this early defense did not embody an integrated view of life which had significance for his initial artistic success—except insofar as his intense insistence on absolute subjectivity and individualistic response, both in his study and his efforts at personal publicity, pointed to their exploration in *Hunger* and Hamsun's evolving aesthetic theories. Instead, the extremity of his views and particularly their deviation from those of such established figures as Bjørnson and Janson seem to have functioned largely as a conscious and self-inflated strategy to wrest attention from the literary mentors of Scandinavia—a technique he subsequently repeated in his aggressive attack on Norway's reigning literary quadrumvirate of Ibsen, Bjørnson, Kielland, and Lie.

But it was the success of *Hunger* and the innovations it heralded in style and content that directed the early course of his artistic unfoldment throughout the nineties and into the twentieth century. Not until the second decade of this century did he emerge as a social critic in his creative writings, in works extending from *Children of the Times* of 1913 through *The Ring Is Closed* of 1936. In these writings his earlier contact with the spiritual and social ramifications of American life in the eighties doubtless helped to isolate and focus his criticism, but his canvas was Norway, not America, a shift in intellectual engagement already evidenced in his 1908 critique of Jensen's book and confirmed by his entire literary production. As the Norwegian critic Reidar Andersen-Næss has recently stated, "Hamsun's writing, as distinctly personal and stubbornly individualistic as it is, has its roots deep in Norwegian life of his age; it is both in its premises and intentions a piece of Norwegian history, both good and bad. Here we meet, as a historical reality and spiritual climate, the total structural change that accompanied the transition from a rural society to an industrial state and that is the sum total of the last one hundred years of Norwegian history, because it more than any political, military, or literary event has intruded upon the life of every single Norwegian."[20]

This, then, was Mark Twain's critic, born 1859, died 1952. Like hundreds of thousands of his countrymen, he sought his fortunes in America only to find authentic fulfillment in his own land.

---

[20] "Landstrykermotivet i Hamsuns diktning," *Nordisk Tidsskrift*, XXXVII (1961), 445.

# The Cultural Life of Modern America

# Preface

Truth is neither two-sided nor objective; truth is precisely disinterested subjectivity.

This book is an expansion of two lectures that I delivered at the Copenhagen Students' Association last winter.

*Knut Hamsun*

*Copenhagen, April 1889*

# The Cultural Climate

## I. Patriotism

The first thing that strikes the travel-weary foreigner in America and makes him bewildered is of course the intense noise, the restlessness, the hectic life in the streets, the nervous, bold dispatch with which things move along everywhere. If he lands in New York in the summertime, he will moreover be a little surprised to see gentlemen without jackets, without vests, with no more than suspenders over their shirts, strolling along the streets, arm in arm with ladies dressed in silk. This immediately has a foreign air, an air of freedom; there is haste in this kind of etiquette. And the pace does not slacken as he travels westward. Everywhere there is the same bustling hurrah in things, the same steam-hammer din, the same clamorous activity in all that goes on. The country is a pioneer society in its earliest days, a whole world in itself, where people are now about to begin living— a society in the making. There is all the feverish rush and to-do that comes of people on the move; every day is moving-in day for a newcomer. Such din and commotion are very natural for a nation that is still only half-settled and still groping in search of a permanent place for itself and its people. But it is this very din and commotion that newspapers and speakers and poets here at home have celebrated as a product of the Republic's free institutions. And Americans themselves are convinced that all this restlessness and energy and incessant whirl are a trait that freedom itself has stamped on the American national character. No question about it; this is the uplifting power of freedom! For two hundred years America has made human beings out of Europe's worst spawn; it has turned idlers from every corner of the earth into steady workers. We have been told wondrous tales about people who went shuffling about in wooden shoes here suddenly becoming light-footed there—and this was due, above all, to the free institutions. No question about it; this was the uplifting power of freedom!

But this explanation of the emigrant's rapid transformation is a bit too idealistic for anyone with experience. There is a far more obvious cause: an economic one. The same family that lived on two crowns a day here needs a dollar and a half a day there, and for the great majority it takes considerable doing to get hold of this dollar and a half; it really keeps you whirling to earn that money. In addition to this, you find yourself in the midst of a foreign land which, however long you live there, remains a foreign land. The entire mode of living in America is so vastly different from what the emigrant is used to at home that he never gets it completely into his blood; he will always feel like a foreigner. But it can make people nervous, and it can make them step lively. People are in a constant state of alarm; they feel pressured by so much that is unfamiliar, astonished by all that is new, confused by all that is strange. They get upset if they are simply going to buy a new pair of shoes, dreading that they may not know enough English to haggle. Their hearts pound even if they no more than get a slip from the city treasurer, and they go tearing off to pay their taxes. Their inner calm is gone, but they have grown active; suddenly they have grown very light-footed. A sojourn in America is very definitely an effective stimulant; people's minds and energy are set in motion. But one grows active and light-footed from the instant one steps ashore and starts to earn money for one's first meal—long before coming into contact with political freedom in the Republic.

The second impression that jolts the foreigner as soon as he has begun to take note of details in this clamorous bustle is the Americans' enormous patriotism. Every so often he encounters a street parade of war veterans, people who are curiously rigged out in multi-colored ribbons, with tiny flags in their hats and brass medals on their chests, marching in step to the hundreds of penny whistles they are blowing. There is absolutely no other point to these parades than an attention-getting march through the streets in step to hundreds of penny whistles—absolutely no other point. This frequently repeated procession is a symbolic expression of the Americans' fervid national feeling. All street traffic ceases while this procession passes by—not even the streetcars are allowed to break through—and people who are busy indoors come streaming out onto the steps to watch this weekly recurring phenomenon. It is quite simply everyone's civic duty to watch this ridiculous parade, without smiling. For the men with the penny whistles are patriots. Just as these soldiers punished the southern aristocrats in the last war for refusing to obey, so the American people today would be prepared to fight if another nation opposed their wishes. It is incredible how naively cocksure Americans are in their belief that they can whip any enemy whatsoever. There is no end to their patriotism; it is a patriotism that never flinches, and it is just as loudmouthed as it is vehement. For some time now the American press has been sternly lecturing England in regard to her fishing treaty with Canada, and I have heard Americans say privately, "Just let England come and try to make something of it—just let her come!" When Lasker, the German national assemblyman and leader of the German national liberals, died some time ago in New York, the American Congress sent a letter of condolence to—Bismarck! Now Bismarck was only human; he was not particularly disposed to grieve himself sick over the death of his most bitter adversary; he just could not understand good Yankee tact; he threw the paper into an envelope and sent it back. But then American patriotism broke loose: Did Bismarck have the nerve to treat their loftiest message like a piece of paper? Well, just let Germany come on—just let her come! At the time American newspapers were full of diatribes against Bismarck. I happened to be doing some traveling at that time, and wherever I went I found that the public was simply gnashing its teeth. A couple of large Eastern papers finally admitted that Congress perhaps had blundered in sending this official condolence to the German government; but the next day the same papers went right back to their original stand.

People had visited them—it turned out that they had lost subscribers between yesterday and today.

American patriotism never tries to avoid a flare-up, and it is fear-
less about the consequences of its hot-headed impetuosity. It is so
arrogant that, in those people who lack a corresponding degree of
intelligence, it becomes a fatuous pride. There is *one* country,
America; anything beyond this is no good. Nowhere on earth is
there such freedom, such development, such progress, and such
intelligent people as in the land of America. A foreigner often feels
wounded by this hulking smugness. Unavoidably he comes up
against situations daily that make him suffer again and again from
the Americans' sweeping sense of superiority. He is bypassed,
laughed at, made a fool of, pitied, and ridiculed. The upshot of this
daily humiliation ultimately is that he himself tries to become an
American as best he can—he tries to "Americanize" himself—an
effort that then earns him the unqualified praise of political candi-
dates on election day. He learns the formal aspects of Americanism
rapidly; he learns to speak English, he learns to wear his hat tilted
over his right ear, he learns to surrender the inside of the sidewalk
to ladies and to conduct himself in every way according to the
external patterns of behavior that characterize the Yankee in his own
land. Then American national pride has reached fulfillment: there
is one more American in America.

But quite often this national pride also assumes very naive forms.
At the same time that the foreigner feels wounded by it, he is also
frequently amazed at the ignorance, the gross unenlightenment on
which this national pride rests. He is surprised to find that a nation
so taken with itself knows so curiously little about others. The very
same thing that Americans are proud of having may very often be
something that is old and familiar in Europe without their knowing
it; not infrequently I have had to put up with their calling Norwegian brooches and German penholders American inventions. I
had a knife with me, the kind that pulls out of a sheath, which
aroused great admiration: out on a farm in Dakota it was a far
greater success than I was. "What won't those goldarn Yankees think
of next!" It took me a week to convince those people that the knife
was a *Swedish* invention.

And this ignorance of others does not exist only in the lower strata of society—not at all; it pervades every social class, all ages, everything. Unfamiliarity with foreign peoples and foreign achievements is one of the national vices of the American people. Americans do not get a comprehensive education in their common schools. The authorized geography in these schools is American geography; the authorized history is American history—all the rest of the world is included in a mere supplement of a couple of pages. People have been very busy promoting the American common schools as model schools. Speakers who have sung America's praises and newspapers that have followed their tune agree fully that the equal of their grade schools does not exist, not in European countries, and that a person can safely bet his life that the American grade schools are without equal. Among other things, it is cited as a unique merit that they are nonconfessional. In the first place, there is no longer anything unique about that; in the second place, the American common schools are *not* nonconfessional. That is not true; it is just the same old song. They do not have religion as a school subject, but ultra-orthodox Christianity is smuggled in at every opportunity; one dogma after another is ladled into the children, one after another, as long as their schooling lasts. I have even seen it happen in an arithmetic period when one of the pupils was caught throwing paper wads: he had no choice but to beg Jesus for forgiveness. What is more, every single morning the instruction in American schools begins with a devotion, with hymns and the recitation of a passage from the Bible. Consequently, people ought to sing very softly about the schools' being nonconfessional.

The greatest negligence of these schools, however, is revealed in their failure to teach children anything about foreign peoples and conditions. American children grow up with no other knowledge of the world than what they have learned about America. Therefore, later on as adults, they are overcome with amazement when they hear that a Swede has invented a sheath knife, and it is thus that American patriotism in many instances becomes so unreasonably cocksure. Then it is not only in the lower strata of society that ignorance is so terribly pervasive—indeed not, but also higher up, high up. I have even found it among the teachers themselves. In 1883 there was a professor at the high school in Elroy, Wisconsin, who was greatly astonished when I told him that we also had the telegraph in Norway—in 1883!—and he was in the habit of scrutinizing the stamps on my letters from home in such a way that I got the feeling he did not believe his own eyes. "You have a postal system in Norway too!" said he. "It is 1883," I answered. This teacher—like the pupils in his school—got his knowledge of Norway from their schoolbook, from a four-page travel account by the American President Taylor, who in the fifties had studied Norway from a cariole.[1]

Knowledge of other nations and peoples is so limited that wherever I have traveled in America the majority of Yankees have as a matter of course called all Scandinavians Swedes. If you live among them for a time, you discover readily, besides, that as soon as you are called a Swede, it is in a pejorative sense, as if you really ought to beg their pardon for being a Swede. There is rarely any use in trying to establish that you are not Swedish at all but rather Norwegian or Danish. As a rule it is quite futile; if you are a Scandinavian, you are a Swede. Nevertheless if it is thus only with indulgence, with a kind of pity, that people call a man from Scandinavia a Swede, it is with absolute contempt that they call a man from France a Frenchman. Among the Yankees, "Frenchman" is an epithet, a term of abuse, corresponding to our word "Turk"; and if one is erroneously accused of being a Frenchman, one must not allow the insult to go uncorrected. In this regard Americans carry on just like the longshoremen at home in Christiania who berate each other with such epithets as "congressman" and "genius." Really, one ought to laugh at this stupidity, one ought to rise above it; but the family provider who is bypassed in his trade *because* he is a Swede, *because* he is a Frenchman, does not laugh. The issue has its serious side. As a Norwegian in America I have had the experience of being taken for a Swede, and as a Swede I have been bypassed, laughed at, made a fool of, pitied, and ridiculed.

In such circumstances, the immigrant undergoes a very natural process in Americanizing himself as quickly as possible; it is a question of his own welfare in the struggle to make a living over there. He hears the superiority of Americans proclaimed so often that finally his sole ambition is to resemble them. His clothes show that he has discarded the old Adam, he even speaks English at home, to his elderly parents no less, who do not understand him, and he tries in everything he does to erase every last trace of his foreign origin. Therefore when a man who once went shuffling around in wooden shoes here comes back from America and astounds his countrymen at home with the marvelous swing to his movements, it is neither the climate that has given him this air nor the republican institutions; it is caused simply and solely by the arrogance of American national pride that for economic reasons has kept him awhirl.

You find even stronger evidence of the immensity of American patriotism in the Congressional debates on immigration restrictions. People are now serious about closing their doors to foreigners, not because this will be necessary for hundreds of years, but simply because the notion is a current fancy, a patriotic caprice. In essence the ban on immigration is an expression of the same American smugness that manifests itself in the Americans' belief that they are superior to Swedes, Frenchmen, and all other foreigners in every field of competition. It is a question of keeping out everything that is un-American; for such things are not good. The excuse has been made that the land is all taken now, that there are enough people now. That is a pretext, a joke. No, it is sheer patriotism that makes Americans want to bar their portals to foreign labor—without which they cannot even get their work done. For Americans do not work. That tale is not true, either. Again it is the same old song. Statistics show that only one fiftieth of the Americans engage in actual manual labor; it is the foreigners who till the land. And these foreigners are the ones whom people now want to shut out "because the land is all taken, because there are enough people."

There are sixty million people in America, whose area is 2,970,000 square miles (excluding Alaska); of this land one and a half million square miles are arable. But of these one and a half million square miles of arable land, only *one ninth* is cultivated; even at that America could export 283,000,000 bushels of grain in the last census year—after its then fifty million people had eaten their fill. And they are not small eaters in America. A Yankee consumes between two and three times as much food as a European and between three and four times as much as a Scandinavian. While the Scandinavian countries have 12 bushels of grain and 51 pounds of meat for each individual per year, America has 40 bushels of grain and 120 pounds of meat for each individual per year.*

If all of America's tillable land were brought under plow, it could feed six hundred million people just on the basis of the estimated yield for the last census year (1879), which was a middling year; and Edward Atkinson, an agriculturalist employed by the United States government, declares in a new work that the American farm that now feeds ten people can easily feed twenty, just by introducing fairly up-to-date production methods, that is, simply by a fairly sensible use of agricultural land. For America's sun is so hot that it ripens fruit in a few days, and America's soil is so rich that one slides in it as in green soap; it can produce a virtually unlimited yield under proper management—something the American farmer does not know how to take advantage of. He uses his land for twenty to thirty years without fertilizing it; he uses seed from his own crops throughout his entire lifetime; he sows wheat in the same fields for ten to twenty years consecutively; he never turns under a meadow, and he never lets a field lie fallow. With somewhat better farm management of America's total plow land, the United States can feed, according to Atkinson's estimate, a population of twelve hundred million—that is just about every human being on the entire face of the earth.

* Mulhal: Balance Sheet of the World, 1870–1880, page 39

| France | 24.02 bushels of grain & | 81.88 lbs. of meat |
|---|---|---|
| Germany | 23.71 " " " " | 84.51 " " " |
| Belgium | 22.84 " " " " | 57.10 " " " |
| Great Britain | 20.02 " " " " | 119.10 " " " |
| Russia | 17.97 " " " " | 54.05 " " " |
| Spain | 17.68 " " " " | 25.04 " " " |
| Austria | 13.57 " " " " | 56.03 " " " |
| Scandinavia | 12.05 " " " " | 51.10 " " " |
| Italy | 9.62 " " " " | 20.80 " " " |
| Europe | 17.66 bushels of grain & | 57.50 lbs. of meat |
| United States | 40.66 " " " " | 120.00 " " " |

So there are not enough people.*

As for the statement that the land is all taken, the land is *not* all taken. That is a pretext and a joke. In the first place, it is "taken" in that stock companies have grabbed up tens of thousands of acres which they do not use but are simply holding on to in expectation of maximum land values. One company has 75,000 acres, another 120,000, etc. So, in fact, this land is not all taken; it is just owned, not used. In the second place, the last census shows that in spite of this method of taking land there was vacant arable public land in nineteen states of the Union; there were 561,623,981 acres of vacant arable public land in these nineteen states. And this colossal expanse of land alone could, according to Atkinson's estimate, feed one hundred million people—at that, they could eat between three and four times as much as in Scandinavia.

So the land is not all taken.

The proposals to restrict immigration rest on shaky ground. They are simply the green fruits of American patriotism; their purpose is to fend off all foreign aid and all foreign influence. They are the result of the Americans' strongly developed celestial belief in themselves, whereby foreign labor can neither be acknowledged as necessary nor recognized as superior to the country's own. American patriotism goes that far; that is how patriotic Americans are. The Congressional committee that appointed itself so that it could get embroiled in multifarious discussions of the restriction issue sent an official letter to the American ministers in every foreign country asking them if indeed it were not both right and proper to close America to foreigners now, if indeed it were not a great patriotic mission they had at hand. And all the ministers in all the countries

* America's mining and manufacturing have not yet been included. America alone produces over half of the world's demand for silver and gold; it has iron mines in twenty-three states; it has rivers of petroleum and there are entire counties of solid coal. While England is hampered by the ever-rising cost of extracting coal from its deep mines, so that in a ten-year period 564 mines have shut down, the United States has enough surface deposits of coal for the whole world for centuries to come. In addition, rivers and lakes full of fish lie along the entire stretch from the Atlantic Ocean to the Pacific coast; every stream contains salmon and whitefish.

swore by Washington and answered saying: "Thou art right! You have it! It is!" The most naive is the United States minister in Venice. After having described the Italian emigrants, their poverty, their rags, he continues verbatim in the following manner: "They (the Italians) are no more fitted to perform the duties of citizenship than slaves newly released from bondage. They have no intention of becoming citizens of the United States. *They desire simply to get more money for their work and to do as little as possible for the pay.*" Those nasty Italians! To this sinister unmasking of the Italian emigrants the periodical *America* adds the following short and pithy editorial comment: "The words of this minister should be firmly engraved on the mind of every patriotic American and remembered as the greatest truth expressed about the greatest evil of our time."*2

The strength and scope of American patriotism are absolutely incomprehensible to those who have not experienced its pressures in their daily lives. It is carried to such extremes that foreigners are compelled to deny their nationality and pose as native Americans whenever they see the chance. For a worker, it is often necessary to be Yankee-born in order to get work, especially the more important positions, such as in banks, in public office, and with the railroads. The only people who have the Americans' respect, in spite of a national animosity stemming from the Revolutionary War, are the English. In many ways America still sees its model and example in England, and the tag ends of the old English civilization are still the latest fashion of the day in modern America. If you want to compliment an American dude, then take him for an Englishman; he lisps like the most splendiferous lord, and when he rides the streetcar he habitually makes the conductor change a gold piece or a large bill.

## II. Hostility to Foreigners

Now what is the state of culture among such people who only know about their own country? What is the intellectual life like in this land that has such patriotic citizens?

* *America*, December 1888.

If America were an old society with a long history behind it—a history that had given the people their characteristic stamp, that, in a word, had endowed the nation with an original intellectual heritage of its own—then perhaps technically America could afford to exclude the outside world and be sufficient unto itself. It would then have a contemporary analogy, for example, in the celestial isolation of Parisian literature. But in a country like America where everything is so torn up and inharmonious, in this pioneer society where no cultural individuality has yet taken root, where no distinctive intellectual character has yet taken shape—in such a country both this self-sufficiency and this self-complacency very seriously impede all recent efforts toward progress. They become a veto, a ban, whose breach does not go unpunished. As a result, you find in this land of America that intellectual products bearing the mark of European influence have been roughly treated by the country's enraged patriots. In 1868 the writer Walt Whitman was dismissed from his post in the Department of the Interior in Washington for committing an act of literary daring in his *Leaves of Grass*—an act so daring that even we here at home are not afraid to commit it in our Christmas tales.[3] That Whitman was later restored to favor and placed in another department did not stem from the fact that people had finally caught sight of his literary merit, but only from their having suddenly remembered that, after all, Whitman had been a nurse, a patriot, in the Civil War. For this he was to be honored, nothing else. Actually he is still in the same disrepute among American literary mentors. He is boycotted; no one buys his books anymore. The seventy-year-old man now lives exclusively on voluntary contributions from England.

In 1878 a young American named Welles published a collection of poems under the title *Bohême*. Welles was quite gifted, a rising lyric poet, a talent of promise, but he was very quickly silenced. It developed that this young man had come under the influence of European literature; his lyrics were an alien, richly poetic challenge to American fair-weather poetastery. He was urged to be silent; great journals urged him to be silent. He had read Shelley, which he ought not to have done, and had learned a bit from Alfred de Musset, which was even worse. No one could fathom how such a strange creature ever found a publisher in the first place.*⁴ That man has simply been rooted out of American literature. Charles Stuart Welles was his name.

It is almost incredible how hard America works at being a world of its own in the world. Just as the country feels it has enough people, it also feels it has sufficient culture, and armed with this sacred conviction it forcibly obstructs all the teeming currents of external intellectual life from streaming in; nowhere does it feel there is any need for modern impulses from foreigners. This does not immediately meet your eye; you do not see it just by passing through. You encounter it in your daily contacts, by attending court sessions and church services, by studying the theater and the literature, by traveling widely, by making your way into their social life, their schools, their families, by reading their papers and listening to their conversations on the streets, by sailing with them on the rivers and working with them on the prairies—only after mingling with them in this way do you get a fairly clear idea of how all-encompassing the Americans' celestial conceit really is. It is reserved for America, where there is a greater crossing of cosmopolitan elements than in any other country in the world, to keep systematically aloof from the modern cultural currents of the outside world. Its culture is marked by age and other nations' use; it is a transmitted culture, introduced into the country by the first colonists—a culture that has seen its day in Europe and is now dying in America. It is the old culture of the English. "Bred in English habits of thought, as most of us are," says an uncommonly self-effacing American author, "we still have not shaped our natures in accord with the new conditions under which we live. Our philosophers have not yet taught us what is best, nor have our poets sung to us what is most beautiful in the life that we live. And therefore we still read the old English wisdom, and still harp upon the antiquated strings."†⁵

The Americans cannot bring themselves to accept new cultural impulses from abroad even in areas where they know that other

---

* I refer, *inter alia*, to the January issue of *International Review*, 1879.
† *Encyclopaedia Britannica*, I, 720.

countries are in the lead. Their sense of honor will not permit them.
Thus the very same thinking that is apparent in the ban on immigration asserts itself also in the import duty that the United States
imposes on art and literature. Last year Europe paid $625,000 for
permission to show contemporary art to the Americans—it paid
2,250,000 crowns. This is the way art is received on the other side
of the ocean, not to mention the even more onerous tariff on modern
literature. At a time when the American Treasury is overflowing
with money which in fact people are at a loss to make use of, the
importation of foreign art, contemporary art, is subject to a 35 percent duty. This is happening at the very moment that American
culture is dying, slowly but surely, slowly but surely of old age. How
could Walt Whitman possibly go scot-free when he had written a
book that contained a human word about a human phenomenon!
And how could Welles write verse influenced by European literature
without being punished! Nevertheless, it is typical that American
tariff laws contain two exceptions to the regulations governing art.
The first—this is characteristic—is of a patriotic nature: American
artists residing abroad can send their works home duty-free. But if
the paintings are framed, they have to pay a special duty on the
frame—for the frames are so infamously foreign. The second exception—this again is characteristic—applies to *antiques*. In 1887 the
Secretary of the Treasury (!) issued a ruling, which was later
affirmed, that paintings dating prior to 1700 can be imported duty-
free—as antiques. This characteristic fact demonstrates just how
eager for progress the Americans really are. The culture to which
America opens its doors is that culture which has become an antique,
culture prior to 1700. As if the Yankees could not also lose their
souls through contact with the bold-spirited art of old.

Under the caption "American" in all our newspapers we are accustomed to reading stories, one more preposterous and fantastic than
another, about American ingenuity in both art and invention. And
we have grown accustomed to looking upon these strokes of genius
that are described there as a natural expression of American intellectual activity and great intelligence. Now the truth is, however,
that the majority of these accounts under the caption "American"

are initially concocted in Europe, so that the American newspapers get them from there. The tale about wealthy American women having small diamonds set in their teeth to enhance the sparkle of their smiles is thus one the New York newspapers first heard about from Belgium, where it appeared in a newspaper under the heading "American." Indeed I am convinced that practically every European newspaper hack remembers how once in his wild and fanciful youth he sat and concocted American wonder tales for his newspaper. It is very convenient to locate a cock-and-bull story in America, that distant land, that remote corner of the world. And Americans themselves are not at all offended by these stories. They look upon them, and rightly so, as advertisements that do not cost them anything, and they really like getting free publicity. The Americans are great advertisers. Even all the noise they make and the frantic pace at which they work are, in the broadest sense, advertisements; nations that advertise less get just as much done with far less clamor and fewer flourishes. The noise is a feature of the American character; it is the whirring wings of publicity.

It is a mistake to regard all those things one hears about from America as fruits of the nation's tremendous development. In reality America is a very backward country culturally. It has energetic businessmen, ingenious inventors, foolhardy speculators; but it has too little culture and not enough intelligence. No doctor's degree is required to become a big-time cattle rancher in Texas, and one need not be able to read a word to make wheat deals on the New York Exchange; the most unintelligent person in the world can have an agent make a bid for him. America's most thriving sector is business—the headlong scramble for profit. And the scramble for profit is not exclusively a modern phenomenon; it is as old as the history of the world. Americans are fundamentally a *conservative* people who in many fields still cling to positions that even Norway, as behind the times as it is, has long since abandoned. This does not apply only to their literature and art but to other facets of their intellectual life as well. They are too self-contained to accept guidance and too patriotic to acknowledge that their country is lagging behind in any way.

Three years ago the American Robert Buchanan wrote a treatise for the *North American Review* in which he sketched a portrait of his countrymen. Because of this he was abused for a year, and people still have not forgiven him. The sketch is five lines long, penned with a heavy heart. His words are all the more telling because he is himself an old man who in his religious beliefs is an ultraconservative and, in his literary tastes, the last great admirer of Longfellow. Even this man found the cultural situation in his country desperate, and he staked his name and reputation to say so. Americans are, he says, "a nation in which the artistic sense is quite dead, a nation which has practically no literature, which is indifferent to all religions, which is corrupt from one end to the other, from the highest pinnacle of public life down to the lowest stratum of society, which is at once thin-skin'd under criticism and bloodthirsty to criticise, which worships the dollar and material power in all its forms, which despises conventional forms and is itself a slave to the most ignoble fashions, which is too hasty to think for itself and therefore lives glibly off the tag ends of second-hand philosophy that is imported from Europe."[*6]

I do not contend that these words are exaggerated; on the contrary, I think they are quite accurate. A way of life has evolved in America that turns exclusively upon making a living, acquiring material goods, a fortune. Americans are so absorbed in the scramble for profit that all their faculties are devoted to it; all their interests revolve around it. Their brains are trained exclusively to grapple with monetary values and columns of figures; their minds like nothing better than what is offered to them by the various financial operations of the moment. The only subject in which their common schools provide daily instruction is arithmetic; figures and statistics are at the core of all their dealings—figures and statistics even drift into ministers' sermons. Figures are used to show what it has cost to save *that* soul living at *that* house number, and the congregation is exhorted to meet that sum. Figures are used to show how great the probability is for Robert Ingersoll's being eternally damned: the sins

* *North American Review*, 1875, I.

committed in his lectures are tallied, and he is also compared with Thomas Paine, who, as everyone knows, did not go to heaven. The Americans' interest in figures is displayed in all their thoughts and actions. Even when they give someone a gift, they expect to be asked what the gift has cost them. When a man gives his fiancée a present, he announces, happy as a god, the price of the present; the greater or lesser value of the gift depends on the price. I was not familiar with this custom during my first stay in America, and when I once—very unexpectedly and, for that matter, very undeservedly —received a gold pen as a gift, people assumed that I did not care about the pen simply because I did not ask the giver what it had cost him. There is really no end to the things whose value Americans appraise in numbers.

On the other hand, there is in America almost no beginning to the things that can *not* be appraised in numbers; there are virtually no new beginnings in American *cultural life*. And how can the Yankees have a modern culture when they cannot bring themselves to accept guidance even in areas where they know that foreign nations are ahead of them? Their notions about love of country will not permit them. Penny-whistle patriotism has permeated their thinking since childhood, transforming a justifiable national pride into a unjustifiable arrogance that nothing and no one can shatter. When all is said and done, it is still the material progress of America that represents the state of its culture, nothing else. Its art, literature, administration of justice, science, politics, or religious practices are not so advanced as to justify its resistance to the cultural products of foreign countries. The republic has acquired an aristocracy with power far exceeding that of the hereditary aristocracies under monarchies; this is the aristocracy of *money*—or more accurately stated, the aristocracy of fortunes, of accumulated capital. For with but a few dollars salted away, the Yankee feels like an aristocrat, just as the newest of barons here at home feels that he belongs to the nobility. This American aristocracy, which the entire nation cultivates with out-and-out religious fervor, has the medieval power of the "true" aristocracy without possessing any of its nobility; crudely and brutally, it is a certain horsepower of economic invincibility.

A European cannot begin to realize the ascendancy of this aristocracy in America any more than he can imagine, even if he knows how powerful money is here at home, the unprecedented omnipotence it has achieved. The ice trusts and coal rings and land-buying and railroad monopolies that we read about in American papers are but the blatant, the exceptional, instances of its power. They are the hurricanes that desolate landscapes but in whose wakes the grass again grows.

But in the conversations of Americans, in the tone of their newspapers, in the atmosphere of their homelife and the nightmare of their thoughts—in *everything* there is the same unyielding, ceaseless craving: for a fortune, for money salted away, for economic nobility. The Americans are a nation of businessmen; in their hands everything turns into a business deal. But they are a nation with little intellectual substance; their culture is sadly empty. Let them be masters of mechanical invention: in the final analysis the invention of machines is an economic question, dependent on a country's resources for broad experimentation; let them have their industries—which incidentally are less national than any other country's—let them also have their commerce, their well-developed banking systems, their admirable communications media; let P. T. Barnum's be an exceptional circus and let the Chicago hog market be the biggest hog market in the world—this is not exactly compelling evidence that a country possesses a culture of the highest order. Americans are not intellectually engaged. They are not remotely intellectually aroused, and for just this reason their business enterprises are so grandiose, so wildly extravagant; the combined manpower of sixty million people is concentrated on the promotion and sale of goods. No wonder then that a cloud of steam trails after America's name throughout the world!

Now it might be objected that, considering the kind of people America has worked with, the country cannot be expected to have made greater headway: it has absorbed and refined the worst elements of every land and made them what they are; it has made human beings of knaves from every corner of the earth—is that not a cultural achievement of the highest order? Indeed it is! I wish to amend this, however, by saying that above all America has made *Americans* out of these knaves; it has incorporated them into a state and made them into citizens; they can become human beings if there is time and opportunity. But try talking to Americans like this and you will hear a thing or two! Say that no one expects America to have achieved a higher cultural standing than it has, or a more intellectual cast than it has, and you will get an answer you will never forget. You will be asked to come and make something of it—just come on! In my own humble way I have tried: I have tried to express my very profound respect for America's ennobling effect upon its citizens, but I stopped. I *had to* stop, for I used to add that one could hardly expect American culture to have yet reached the heights of the age. With that I touched off a frenzy of patriotism, and I stopped talking. I wanted to hold on to my head, I wanted to live. I could mention the time and place on the Dakota prairies when it was nip and tuck with my scalp because I made excuses for the outmoded intellectual outlook in America. For a Yankee, America is the world. He recognizes absolutely no superiority in a foreign nation. To excuse him for not having achieved a higher degree of intelligence is thus in his eyes to excuse him for having reached the *highest* degree of intelligence. What nation, what foreigner, can compare with him? In the summer of 1887 I was working at a place far out in the West; all in all there were perhaps fifty men at the place. On Sundays I was put to writing letters for these people; I was compelled to—they thought I wrote so well. But could I do stenography? I could not? Well, then, they would just like me to know that there were people in America who could write as fast as people talk, for they had seen it themselves. So I was beaten in writing too. I have already mentioned that people on the prairies are not the only ones who are uninformed about the notable things—including stenographers—that other countries also have to offer; this complete ignorance about the outside world is present in every class and in all sections of this country with the model schools.

There is no use trying to excuse the undeveloped state of American intellectual life or to make allowances for the unsuitable material from which the Americans have had to shape their culture. They demand unqualified recognition as the most advanced nation in every field, as the nation with the greatest cultural riches in the world. In order to let others know of this conviction, they declare all foreign influence superfluous to the needs of their intellectual life, and they set up the most severe countermeasures against this influence; they encumber the cultural products from abroad with a 35 percent duty.

# Literature

## I. Journalism

Can American art and literature afford to live under the tariff burden imposed on foreign art and literature? Can it with impunity dispense with artistic influence from abroad?

If America were an old society with historic greatness and an artistic past behind it, were it a country with distinguished ancestors to fall back on, then this restriction would be technically well founded, if unwarranted. But it must be remembered that America is a pioneer society in the making—a society that has not yet founded its own school in any one of the arts. Americans are business people but not creative artists—with exceptions, of course. They charge admission to look at art; they do not understand art; they are indifferent to art. The case is about the same with literature. Just as Americans perceive a mixture of colors in genuine art, which is also what they can see in oleographs, they are completely indifferent to the artistic quality of a book as long as it contains romance and shooting. Literature is not a force in America; it is not an educational medium, but only a more or less diverting amusement. People do not read as a means of personal development but to be amused by the street argot of the popular ballads, to be titillated by the scenes of bloodshed in detective stories, to be moved to tears by the passionate love in Charlotte Braeme's novels, to be lulled to sleep by great sleepy Longfellow. Americans read the newspapers in order to stay abreast of the happenings in town and to keep an eye on the outcome of the latest racing event in New York or to learn a bit about Jay Gould's most recent railroad swindle; they do not read them for word of the latest trends in literature and art, or in the sciences either, for such things are not in the newspapers. The principal content of American papers is business and crime.

The newsboy in an American town is a useful guide and gauge of culture. If you, as a foreigner, study his shouts for a week, you will have the key to life in his town. He is the professional sensor of the public mood, the barometer of its climate. In hawking his papers he knows exactly how to appeal to the prevailing interests of the people; he does not advertise a book, a painting, or a play when he knows that the public is interested in train accidents and triple murders. Now since the papers in America are business enterprises first of all, and since they earn more on triple murders than on culture and intellect, their content is determined accordingly. So when a newsboy shouts about the fire on Washington Avenue, the fight on 17th Street, the snowstorm in Montana, and the rape in Massachusetts, he is calling out the major subjects of his paper. It is thus the lowly newsboys, their opinions in turn shaped by the prevailing interests of the public, who are the controlling editors in American journalism.

A peculiar journalism, a noisy, scandal-hungry, wild and clench-fisted, gun-smoking journalism with bribed editorials, paid publicity for the railroads, advertising poetry, town gossip. A peculiar journalism, with scandals from the law courts, human misery from train collisions, hurrahs from patriotic banquets, steam-hammer blows from the great factories, the word of God from the paper's staff minister—for a paper has a minister on its staff—female poetry about moonshine in Tennessee and love in Boston, two columns of adultery, three columns of bank swindles, four columns of patent medicine. A peculiar journalism, with the clamor of that whole army of powder-blackened pirates who write it.

In a lecture on Sunday papers, the nationally known Brooklyn minister De Witt Talmage recently made the following statements about the American press in general: "It has settled down. And reformers in and out of journalism should redouble their efforts to-

ward making it better and better, raising its morality, and causing it
to become a medium of accomplishing much good. Our newspapers
have more than kept pace with the world. Compare one of our average daily papers of to-day with one from thirty-five years ago, and
you are surprised at the great progress it contains in the direction
of better and better literature. The men who are employed upon
newspapers to-day are better men than the journalists of thirty-five
years ago. Their productions are more healthy, and the tone of the
secular press has already become increasingly religious and moral.
Morality in the newspaper is as good as morality in the pulpit. Yes,
the press has settled down."

But since Pastor Talmage is not known for his sense of humor and
since the man is devoid of irony, even the Yankees felt that he was
bragging about things that he knew nothing about, and some journalists came to the defense of their departed predecessors. Accordingly the editorial staff of *America* answered the pastor with an
indignant five-line article, in which they took exception to Talmage's
good faith in the current morality of the American press. In its
entirety, the article is as follows: "If you compare one of our *Sunday
papers* of to-day to an average *daily paper* of thirty-five years ago, you
will find that the latter was moral in its tone and patriotic in its content, while the former is a hodgepodge of vileness, sensation, and
scandal, merely glossed over with seriousness. The morality of the
Sunday newspapers may be the equal of that of the pulpit, but this
is a very woful confession from the mouth of a minister."[1]

The content of American journalism, however, does not suffer
from any "better literature" than it readily can stand. It is a journalism which, from a literary standpoint, can only be compared to the
small Copenhagen newssheets; it is a boulevard commodity whose
spirit and content throughout are determined by America's own
materialistic climate. In America, if Modjewska has appeared at
the Grand in town, if Menter has played in opera, or Linde has
given a reading, such events will have completely lost their interest
by the next day; and if the morning papers mention them, it is primarily to describe the performers' costumes and hairstyle, to indicate the number of rings on their fingers, the number of their

curtain calls, and to estimate in round figures the price of their jewelry. Do not look for an account of their art, a description of their performance, a detailed critical review, a spirited comment; this is not in the newspapers. Whom would this review be written for? And who would write it? The journalists are trained by the newsboys who in turn are raised by the great newspaper-buying public, and the great newspaper-buying public consists of people who are not interested in art. They are businessmen who enjoy their paper on the streetcar as they ride to work in the morning or businessmen's wives and daughters who have attended the performance themselves and consequently have seen Modjewska's hairstyle with their own eyes. No, give them the bloody mutilation of a corpse that has been found in an entryway, give them the play of wild chance on the stock exchange, a major strike, the latest marriage drama. This they understand; it appeals to their mentality and at last makes a dent in their callousness.

Amid this hubbub of business, crime, and accidents, each American newspaper devotes one or two columns of news to domestic life in the community—the editor's intimate reports dug up at second and third hand, the ladies' morning reading, the scholarly source material of idlers—the so-called "locals." In these columns you learn of marriages, births, and deaths; and just as European newspapers report that such and such princely personages are visiting this or that princely family for political reasons, so American newspapers carry an announcement in their locals when an esteemed family in town is visited by an esteemed fellow being from another town. It may be a skipper's wife from the Lakes who has come to see her son who is a wheelwright, or it may be a cattle herder from the prairies who is visiting his parents—everyone is included, everyone is equally noteworthy. To be sure, there is nothing to be said against this; it is customary in the country, and the ten thousand subscribers accept the fact that the wife of a skipper makes the news. The locals are the quietest spots in an American newspaper; insofar as possible, they are free of patent medicines and crime stories, and they are especially cherished reading for society women. But now and then the noise also breaks into these columns: advertisements are smuggled

into the locals, advertisements for this kind of hair oil and that kind
of corset, verses about toilet articles and verses about a fresh supply
of beef at the bazaar. Right after a story about a spectacular wedding
or an extraordinarily fortunate birth, there can be a notice under
the caption "Death." It gives you a jolt, an absolutely unbearable
jolt—again a beloved Yankee compatriot has passed away. It may
very well be Fowler the bricklayer or a niece of Brown the watch-
maker living at 16 or perhaps 17 Adams Street. Oh, there are no
words powerful enough to express *whom* death can snatch away!
However, you pull yourself together and read on in the notice;
gradually you begin to breathe more easily and in fact you manage
to keep your head. It is not the bricklayer after all, thank goodness,
and when you look more closely, perhaps it is not the niece either.
You cannot complain if it is only an insignificant sewing-machine
agent from Seaside Avenue or even a male cousin of a Mrs. Kingsley,
whose husband is approaching forty. And you go on reading. You
have read halfway through the item; you are growing calmer; you
are really not too far from imagining a man by the name of Conway,
who could perhaps just as well live on Lincoln Street as any place
else. You read along with relish; truly, this is getting interesting.
From this moment on you could forgo reading anything but death
announcements. Of course, as it turns out, the entire notice is just
about an ordinary carpenter whose name is perhaps not far from
being Grimshaw or Smith even. In addition, he maybe died of a
stroke, a cause of death that is right in keeping with the combative
life the man may have led. And you start reading again; you are
very tense and you do not miss a word; you read on feverishly, at
last in sheer frenzy. The carpenter is still safe. There are four lines
left; you have arrived at the final period and not a word about the
stroke! Now could it possibly be a Mr. Downing, perhaps James
William Downing, who might for instance be a barber in the neighborhood of one of the Baptist churches? You steel yourself; in great
agitation you almost decide in favor of such a barber. After all, it
has to be someone and why not a barber just as well as a woman
who runs an oyster shop on Franklin Avenue? Is there any particular
reason for your sparing all the barbers in creation from their fate?

Then at last you read the following, wide-eyed, with bated breath and every nerve quivering with emotion: *In order to escape Death, you must visit the only place in town where you can get Ball's famous gloves in which you never catch your death of cold, that is, at Donaldson's.* Great merciful heavens! The poor reader has enjoyed half a column of advertisement.

Advertisements in the locals are certain to be read; in these columns they do not elude the inquisitive eye. Therefore the locals are expensive advertising space: an eight-point line may cost a dollar —on special occasions, such as holidays, an eight-point line may cost as much as five dollars in the metropolitan locals. Now it is possible for an editor to write the following in his local: "Last night my wife gave birth to a son." Fine; that is interesting, remarkable, sublime! But farther down, in a different item, he thanks an esteemed farmer because he has been to town and presented the editor with a certain quantity of potatoes. This is all just business, just publicity. In return for these potatoes, the editor has to thank the farmer publicly with a brief editorial notice—and right in the local where it is absolutely certain to be read. He has to indicate what *kind* of potatoes they were and what he thinks of them. He has found these potatoes to be so superb that he is convinced that, because of them, his wife was happily and successfully delivered of a son; indeed he is very inclined to believe that had his wife not eaten two of these well-nigh unique potatoes the day before, the child would not have been a boy. The purpose has been accomplished, to be sure, at the expense of serving up and besmirching the most intimate aspects of family life: the editor has free potatoes for a certain length of time and the farmer gets his produce publicized in such a way that it will never be forgotten. The farmer looks at it like this: later on when an unmarried housewife is out of potatoes in her cellar, she will pat her lover on the cheek and say: *"That* kind of potatoes, if you please! You know, the kind that boys come from." Even if she says it jokingly, the farmer figures it still shows that his advertisement in the local—that costly advertisement—has not been forgotten.

As unintelligent, as tough and crude, as American journalism appears, it is still the most accurate expression of the nation's community life, of the people's interests and general notions—which is far more than can be said about the remaining literature in America, its serious literature. The journalists, after all, deal with life as it is; they interpret the Yankee's thoughts and feelings, portray the nation's brawny materialism without embellishment, and make daily contributions to their country's cultural history. The American writers, on the other hand, are still puttering with the outmoded patterns of thought and sentiment that belong to bygone centuries, singing of a mighty love that smacks of the Englishman's grandfather, and making heroes—heroes of humanity—of every single patriotic Yankee who has but a dollar salted away and a sawmill on the Mississippi.

Nor do the American newspapers carry on the comic cavil with politics that the European press is so full of. The Americans battle about free trade and tariff bills for only two or three weeks every fourth year. People fight until the blood flows; they win or lose, they elect a president—whereupon everything is put aside until the next election year. People do not discuss "politics" throughout the four years. The American journalist is spared from having, as a grown man, to sit and fight with enthusiasm about paragraphs in an old law and commas in a new, from having to compose long "leaders" about young Bismarck's rude behavior at the Vatican, from having to work up learned commentaries on throne speeches and royal nonsense. He is acquainted with that kind of politics only by name; he does not know what Liberal and Conservative are—except at election time he does not even know who the opposition is. His paper is dull reading, a conglomeration of incidents from America's East and West, brief treatments of everything, products of the moment.

I have at hand the most recent American dailies—I make no selection—I am taking an issue at random. It contains the following: Arrested Fugitive—Fire Last Night—Lynch Justice—The Consequences of Immigration—The Canadian Fishing Question—Big Fight—Treasury Reserves—The Stock Exchange—Northwestern Opinion—Southern Opinion—Latest News—Visited by Thieves—

From the Supreme Court—Struck Dead—The Only Remedy
(about a patent medicine)—Stolen Lead Pipes—Robbed of $1,000
—Boxers Killen and McCaffrey at the Comique—White Slavery in
Texas—Yesterday's Races—Sports—Was It a Stabbing?—Minne-
sota—Dakota—Michigan—From Other Places—Sudden Death—
Civil Service—Travelers—A Funeral in Winona—Railroad Condi-
tions—Conditions for Railroad Workers—From the Lower Court—
Robbed of Eight Thousand—G.A.R. (Grand Army of the Republic)
—Senator Quay's Lawsuit—Central African Traffic in Women—
Falling Wheat Prices—A Rival's Black Deed—The New York
Market—The Chicago Market—A Negro Backs into Eternity—
Why She Was a Heroine—Bank Clerk's Disappearance—Ministers'
Agreement—Train Derailed—Plant Discovery (a patent medicine)
—Sheriff Eagle's Opinion—Sheriff Cobden's Opinion—Locals—
Deserted Her Husband—Two Firemen Killed—Indians in Peru—
The Legislature—Surprised by Wife—General Grant as Hunter—
Streetcar Conditions—Snowstorms—Sixty-Three-Year-Old Father
Guilty of Immoral Behavior toward His Seven-Year-Old Daughter
—Women's Association—Look to the Birds of the Heavens (adver-
tisement)—A Bankruptcy—Telegrams—How to Dress Smartly—
Murdered Farmer—Powderly Improving—Pastor Fitzgerald's Ser-
mon—Poles Arrested—Go On (concerns ridding the country of
Chinese)—Strike—Gladstone on American Inventions—New
Church Consecrated—Windowpane Broken—Runaway—Three
Policemen on Guard—eleven columns of advertisement.*[2]

Not one word about politics, not one word! But each item—as
unintelligent and uninteresting as they all are—reveals what occu-
pies the minds of the Yankees, what is on their lips, what they feel
like reading. There is a close correspondence between American
newspapers and American intellectual life; their content is not so
demure and idyllic as that of serious literature, but they contain a
hundred times more reality and truth. The American newspapers
are restless and noisy, like life itself. They are raw and true to life.

In one respect the American press is ahead of every other coun-

* *Globe,* January 9, 1889.

try's, that is, in running down and publishing the news with lightning speed. It expends huge sums of money to get information from
everywhere; it permits wires about the most insignificant events, and
it puts out extras at the slightest opportunity. The *New York Herald*
is without equal in this respect. Not counting correspondents in
every country or typesetters, press operators, proofreaders, etc., the
*Herald* has sixty-five men on its permanent staff. Of these, seventeen are editors or chiefs, each running his own special desk; the
rest are reporters who rove the streets and alleys of New York gathering the news. As soon as a piece of news reaches the ears of such a
reporter, he races to the nearest telephone station on the street,
shouts *"Herald!"* and reports in. Besides these reporters, the *Herald*
has its own cutter that plies the waterways of New York, capturing
all the news that can reach the giant city by sea. As is well known,
the *Herald* correspondent had arrived at Niagara and was monopolizing the wires because the Prince of Wales, who was traveling in
America, had decided to visit the waterfalls. Now the prince failed
to show up when expected, but in order to keep his position the
correspondent issued orders to wire the Book of Genesis. When this
was dispatched and the prince still had not arrived, the Book of
Exodus was begun. But then finally the prince came, and the correspondent was the first to send his news out into the world; the ma-
neuver merely cost a few thousand dollars. That was not the first
time the *Herald* managed to steal a march on every other paper with
its news: for instance, during the war in Abyssinia, when even the
*London Times* had to get several of its war dispatches from American
colleagues in what, to top it all off, was a purely English affair.

The *New York Herald* is not the only paper that makes such an
effort to surprise its readers with world-wide news coverage; most of
the American press is in more or less active contact with both inland
cities and foreign countries. It is extremely commendable that the
American newspapers try year after year to give the Yankees some
small knowledge of that world which does lie outside America and
about which their schools provide almost no instruction. To be sure,
foreign coverage in American papers is as a rule confined to brief or
relatively brief cables, but they are nonetheless tidings from another

hemisphere—small, scattered facts which, when gathered together day after day over a period of years, constitute a far more comprehensive history of the world than what any of the country's free schools have to offer. But the American spirit has been decisive in determining the content of these cables, too. The papers have to consider the tastes and interests of their subscribers. Whereas they mention nothing about art or literature, there is not a thing in the financial sector, for example, that is too insignificant to warrant a cable. For American newspapers, court balls, throne speeches, the travels of emperors, the opening of railroads, turf events in England, duels in France, and assassinations in Russia are prized material for cables; but they remain absolutely silent about even the most celebrated drama or the newest outstanding performer in the arts. On the other hand, they immediately send word of the most inconsequential event abroad if it even seems to touch on business and commerce—if a traveler loses his billfold in a German hotel or a man speculates in a cruse of oil on the stock exchange in Sarepta.

Despite its profound shortcomings, American journalism is still the most distinctive and vigorous intellectual manifestation of the American people. In its boldness, its realistic intensity, it is also from a literary standpoint the most modern.

## II. WRITING AND WRITERS

American literature is hopelessly unreal and meagerly endowed. It has romance and shooting, but it does not have life's own dynamic vitality. It is without life's flushed abundance; it does not stir the emotions. I exclude of course those few writers whose books a modern reader finds bearable. I exclude Mark Twain, that pale pessimist, who with his truly sublime humor and wit has no predecessor and no successor in America. I exclude a little of Poe, a little of Hawthorne, a little of Harte. But American literature, by and large, is not the expression of American *life* that the newspapers are. It makes no impression; it is too little of this world; it prates too much and feels too little; it contains too much fiction and too little reality; it does not portray, it praises; it speaks with eyes turned heavenward; it fiddles with virtue and Boston morality; it preaches, admonishes, and puts a Morocco binding around unswerving fidelity and a heroic Indian couple. It is a literature that has passed through my mind without a sound, that has never struck an emotional chord or made me listen. With a Yankee book in hand, you always have the feeling that if a hurricane were to come along, a gust of modernity through this poetic wretchedness, it would help. But there is a duty on hurricanes, and hurricanes do not whistle the national tune. American literature is completely untouched and untouchable. It lies three whole evolutionary stages behind European literature. Dickens and Scott have once and for all determined the nature of its novel, Milton and Longfellow the nature of its verse, and there it stands. American literature does not show any trace of influence from our present-day literature. No thirst for development burns in these poets; they have learned their craft once and for all, and they know their craft. What do they care that there are men in the great civilized lands who have thought of writing about life, that there are others who have begun to depict the mimosa-like stirrings of the human psyche? It does not concern them at all; they are Americans, they are patriots, they are singers, dreamers. Now it is practically a disgrace in America to know a foreign language. If two immigrants converse in their native tongue in the presence of a Yankee, they are ridiculed; if an American learns a foreign language, it is preferably a dead one. Thus Americans are cut off from reading modern literature in the original. And they do not even try to get acquainted with modern literature through translations. If they translate a work of Zola's as a speculation, they mutilate the book brutally—they "sift" it, to use the expression in the foreword. It becomes unrecognizable; even the names of the characters are changed. Thus Jesus Christ in *La Terre* is called Mohammed in the American translation. The translator has spared the four murders in the book, for these are akin to all the shooting in his own literature; but all the swearing, the illegitimate child, and the seductions have been eliminated entirely. Nor are translations of Zola's books, for example, available in bookstores, even in "sifted" form;

they belong in cigar stores—as "articles for men." American book-stores carry on a respectable business. Do not ask for books por-traying real life, do not even insist on the highly temperate and tiresome books of Whitman—it will be whispered in reply, if there are ladies present, that one would hope Whitman's books are not available in town.

What then do these bookstores have to offer? Take a city like Minneapolis, a city the size of Copenhagen, a center of commerce in the West—Minneapolis with its theaters, schools, "art galleries," university, international exhibition, and five music academies. There is one bookstore—a single, solitary one.* What does this bookstore advertise, and what does it have in its windows and on its shelves? Decorated congratulatory cards, gilt-edged collections of verse, de-tective stories, some sheet music for "Yankee Doodle Dandy" and "Home Sweet Home," dear and departed Longfellow, and all the variations of the latest inkwells. Then there is that whole deluge of "fiction" that belongs to a large nation with aspiring female scrib-blers. Now the bookstore is also a patriotic bookstore: it has the histories of United States wars and lithographs of Washington; it has *Uncle Tom's Cabin* and General Grant's memoirs. And then it has all of America's magazine literature.

Now I would still rather read a collection of sermons than Grant's memoirs. Grant was a man who could not even write his own language correctly; several of the general's letters are preserved as stylistic curiosities. I would also rather read the city directory from cover to cover than these American detective stories. They are worse than the "popular ballads," worse than the "letters to heaven," worse than anything I have ever seen in print. If you have never examined them, you have no idea what these detective stories have to offer. However, these literary products are also just as patriotic as any national anthem. In most instances there is a young Yankee lad of sixteen or seventeen from the New York detective division who has discovered and shot down a whole band of foreign Jewish peddlers.

* There are two Scandinavian ones, selling stationery and collections of sermons.

As for American magazine literature, it is a literature with admirably executed illustrations. For people who are fond of pictures, almost any of the large American magazines are a pleasure to leaf through. Their great merit lies in their format and their excellent illustrations; otherwise their content more rarely interests anyone except Americans, real Americans. It is almost impossible to pick up one of these journals without running across a letter from Grant, a Lincoln autograph, an anecdote about Washington, some very important opinion of General Logan's—a man about whom one knows that he is dead and that is all one knows about him—a verse about the moon, a love story. Now in order to read a Lincoln autograph that has already been printed a hundred times or one of Franklin's wise replies to an English lord that we in Norway read in Jensen's *Reader* when we were little or a letter from Garfield to a niece of some farmer in Illinois—in order even to bother reading such things one's mentality has to be completely in tune with the Americans'; one has to be just as intellectually unoccupied as they are.

Minneapolis—the city the size of Copenhagen—also has an atheneum with a library that contains 15,000 volumes and cost $26,000. At this atheneum you again encounter the same literature as in the bookshop—the same war histories, the same magazines, the same Grant, the same verse. The only literature the bookshop has that the atheneum does not is inkwells; otherwise it is complete. People can sit in this atheneum the whole, livelong day and read verse. Really, for a foreigner it is absolutely inscrutable how people can find enjoyment sitting there reading that verse. Apparently it comes from their general predilection for lyric poetry, for it cannot be the quality of this poetry that attracts them to the atheneum. Americans are extremely fond of verse. Not only are there all those ladies who regularly supply the newspapers with their often extremely curious poems; even the most level-headed druggist is seized by poetic madness so that he quotes poetry in a debate on codliver oil—I have seen it in print. Indeed, even Henry George begins his great work on political economy with some verse. You cannot carry it much further; beyond this there is just no place to go. The Minneapolis atheneum has enough verse for the city from now till eternity, and new purchases are being made constantly. What else are they buying? What modern literature does the atheneum have? Every book penned by an American writer, male or female, every novel by Dickens and Scott, Dumas *père*, Eugène Sue, Jules Verne, Marryat, and Silvio Pellico. There is not one book by Zola, none of Bourget, none of the Goncourts, none of the Russian writers, none of the Scandinavian,* not a single book by those men who are the vanguard of literature today. There are a hundred huge volumes of old Congressional debates; there are 83 volumes of back issues of almanacs; there are 670 volumes of patent reports which are twice as thick as Luther's translation of the Bible. Indeed, if you went down to the Minneapolis atheneum and, wishing to read something, you requested a patent report, you would get it. But if you asked the librarian for Hartmann, Comte, or Schopenhauer, the librarian would explicitly draw your attention to the fact  that, of philosophers, he had Emerson.

However critical one may be of American journalism, it still contains the poetry of life in comparison to the country's serious literature; it is a vent for all the noises of America. Every day it dins into your ears the life stories of people who work and people who suffer and people who fall and people who die; it expresses the temper of that whole hemisphere. You must not seek life's shifting multiplicity among the poets; they sing about the moon and shoot Jewish peddlers. More than half of American writing consists of verse. And why not? One ought to acknowledge each product of every mental state in every form if it but shows talent. But let there be some slight meaning in the verse now and again, some slight artistry in the verse from time to time, a spark of human life in one instance out of one hundred! People do not play the lyre in America—perhaps they did so once—they trample it, and the few who play, play badly and they have such poor lyres. But do we not have translations of good things from America, good verse, good Indian poetry? I have stayed with Indians; twice I lived in their wigwams for some time. I did not find a greater number of heroic qualities in the men or greater beauty

* With the exception of some of Andersen's fairy tales and two of Lie's earliest books.

in the women than would fill a short newspaper article—and then just barely. The notion of great Indian poetry is an extremely naive lie; it is just talk, a fiction. Besides, if we are going to talk about translations, it should be noted that at times we do translations more by *countries* than by literatures; what I mean is that a competent writer in a large country finds it far easier to be translated than a quite outstanding writer in a small one. Every literature has translations of such national representatives. Hence we translate B. Peres Galdós because he is a Spaniard, and we translate Hoa Tsien Ki because he is a Chinese.* But often we do not translate Zola, in spite of his being a Frenchman.

But does not America have *Uncle Tom's Cabin?* It is true that this book has performed a real mission on earth. As a literary product, as a novel, it is scarcely even worth the expensive binding it is given in America, but as a piece of polemical writing, as a sermon, as a contribution to the ferment of the day, it has attracted attention as it deserves to do. In spite of its literary worthlessness, it nevertheless seizes hold of the reality of life, and therefore just this very book ought to be a warning to American poets against their moonshine and their make-believe representations of the life people live. But it is not. On the contrary, people are well on the way to making *Uncle Tom's Cabin* itself into a moon legend. The author suggested several years ago—that is, before she became sick—that she did not deserve the honor for *Uncle Tom's Cabin:* an angel, extremely well versed on Negroes, had written the book; she herself had but taken it down. Now let us hope that the angel does not also disclaim authorship! All honor to *Uncle Tom's Cabin.* But it drums my ears a little too full of the yammer of Bostonian morality and Missourian inhumanity. And if a nation points to that book as a typical product of its literary creativity, then things do not look good for that nation: there is too little stirring in mind and heart.

American literature is also, of course, an exceedingly respectable literature—as straitlaced as Norwegian Marie. The Boston clergy has it in its vise; Boston, you see, is the source of America's intellec-

* That we also translate Tcheng Ki Tong is explained by the fact that this writer delineates a culture—in contrast to the above, who is *not* a creative artist.

tual tone, and literature takes its pitch from that city. Without exception, you do not find a single word of honest-to-goodness profanity even among the greatest American writers. A book with one word of profanity would immediately go to the cigar store. In every Yankee novel there is a villainous blackguard; now when this villain is called upon to swear, he expresses the word *hell* as *h* with a dash, the word *damned* as *d* with a dash. I am not trying to say that profanity is an essential ingredient in a good novel, but it seems rather unnatural to me for a villainous blackguard to go around talking in dashes. Nor does American literature know anything about sex. Far from it. It knows much more about Judgment Day and spectrum analysis than about sex. If by chance the old Adam comes out in a fictional character, he appears in the nice, sugar-coated sensuality of a glance or of a kiss, never as an overwhelming force, never as the demanding passion of youth; Boston's vise is clamped around his neck. While American newspapers are flooded every single day with stories of crime and rape, serious literature is almost forbidden to display a naked chair leg.

Now it goes without saying that among American writers as well there are necessarily more or less talented exceptions to the general rule of talentlessness. I have called Mark Twain an exception—I do so again. He is not a creative artist at all, but he is the cleverest wit in American literature—a wily wag who gets people to laugh while he himself sits sobbing; he is a pessimist, humorist, satirist. You have to have participated in American life for a while really to understand all his jabs; they are countless. Among other writers I would not venture to call any author a total exception, just a chapter of one, a verse of another. Only a couple of American literary figures, whose names have become fairly well known here at home, need to be mentioned briefly in passing.

In 1885 a book was published in Boston that generated a letter from Emerson, a reprint in London, and a treatise by Rudolf Schmidt. The book was called *Leaves of Grass* and its author, Walt Whitman. When this book was published Whitman was thirty-six years old.

The author himself calls this work songs; Rudolf Schmidt also calls it songs. Emerson on the other hand, because of his negligible methodical sense, has obviously been unable to hit on any designation for this work. Nor is it in reality songs, any more than multiplication tables are songs. It is composed in pure prose without any meter at all and without rhyme; the only thing that is suggestive of poetry is the fact that one line may have one, two, or three words, the next twenty-eight, thirty-five, or quite literally up to forty-three words.

The author calls himself a "fact of world dimensions"; Rudolf Schmidt also calls him a "fact of world dimensions." I, on the other hand, because I really find it extremely difficult to associate anything with a concept so superbly all-encompassing, so that it might for that matter just as well be the cosmos, outer space, or the universe —I will in all modesty simply call Walt Whitman a *primitive*.[3]

He is the sound of nature in a virgin, primordial land.

There is an Indian cast to both his language and his sensibility; consequently it is primarily the sea, the air, the earth, the trees, the grass, the mountains, the rivers—in short, the natural elements— that he celebrates. He always calls Long Island, which is his birthplace, by its Indian name *Paumanok*; he repeatedly calls corn by its original Indian name *maize* instead of the English word *corn*; again and again he rechristens American places, even entire states, with Indian names; there are entire stanzas in his poems that are composed of names native to America. He is so enthralled with the primitive music of these place-names that he crams in long series of them even in places where they do not have the slightest connection with the text; he often runs through a score of state names without saying a word about the states. A pretentious sport with wild words. One of his poems goes like this:

From Paumanok starting I flew like a bird,
Around and around to soar to sing the idea of all,
To the north betaking myself to sing there arctic songs,
To Kanada till I absorbed Kanada in myself, to Michigen then,
To Wisconsin, Iowa, Minnesota, to sing their songs [. . .]
Then to Ohio and Indiana to sing theirs, to Missouri and
    Kansas and Arkansas to sing theirs,

To Tennessee and Kentucky, to the Carolinas and Georgia
  to sing theirs,
To Texas and so along up toward California, to roam accepted
  everywhere;
To sing first [. . .]
The idea of all the states, the Western world one and
  inseparable (?),
And then the song of each member of these States.[4]

The natural primitiveness in his makeup, his sense of kinship
with the surrounding elements, like that of the wild savage, reveals
itself everywhere in his book, often with blazing prominence. When
the wind sighs or an animal calls, it is as if he heard a series of
Indian names. "The sound of rain and wind," he says, "calls of birds
and animals in the woods, sound like names to us, Okonee, Koosa,
Ottawa, Monongahela, Sauk, Natchez, Chattahoochee, Kaqueta,
Oronoco, Wabash, Miami, Saginaw, Chippewa, Oshkosh, Walla-
Walla . . . giving water and land names."[5] It takes at least twice as
much inspiration to read such verse as to write it.

His style is not English; his style does not belong to any civilized
language. His style resembles the unwieldy pictorial language of
the Indian minus the pictures, influenced by the unwieldy form
and language of the Old Testament which surpass all understanding. His language rolls ponderously and obscurely across the page;
it goes rumbling along in columns of words, regiments of words,
each new one making the poem more unintelligible than the last.
He has poems that are absolutely monumental in their unreadability.
In one of them, an unusually profound poem in three lines of which
more than half is in parentheses, he "sings" as follows:

Still though the one I sing,
(One, yet of contradictions made,) I dedicate to Nationality,
I leave in him revolt, (O latent right of insurrection! O quench-
  less, indispensable fire!)[6]

This could just as well be a birthday greeting as an Easter hymn.
It could also just as well be a poem as a problem involving the rule

of three. But as long as possible you fend off the thought that the author of this calendar-stick poetry has meant to sing that he is a patriot, to be sure, but pretty rebellious too.

O'Connor says you have to have seen Whitman in order to understand his book; Bucke and Conway and Rhys also say that you have to have seen him in order to understand his book.[7] Well, then, it strikes me that the impression of a bemused primitive that you get from reading *Leaves of Grass* is strengthened rather than weakened by a close look at the author. He is, after all, the last gifted specimen of a modern who was born a primitive.

Thirty or forty years ago people in New York, Boston, New Orleans, and later Washington could meet a man on the streets who had an unusually powerful build, a big, quiet man, rather large and heavy of limb, always dressed in a careless manner suggesting a mechanic or seaman or grand laborer of one kind or another. He almost always went without a coat, often without a hat; in hot weather he preferred to stay on the sunny side of the street and let the sun beat down on his great head. His features were massive but handsome; his face had at once a proud and appealing expression; his blue eyes were gentle. He frequently spoke to passersby whether he knew them or not; sometimes he would pat strangers on the shoulder. He never laughed. Mostly he wore gray clothes, which were always clean but often had buttons missing; he wore colored shirts and a white paper collar around his neck.

This is the way Walt Whitman looked at that time.

Now he is a sick old man of seventy. I have seen a picture of him from a number of years back. As usual he is sitting in his shirt sleeves; inappropriately as usual, he has his hat on this time. His face is large and handsome; a great head of hair and a beard he never cuts flow down over his shoulders and chest. On the forefinger of his extended hand he is holding a delicately fashioned butterfly with outstretched wings; he is sitting there watching it.

These portraits of Walt Whitman still do not civilize his book; as a literary endeavor it is sheer poetic dissonance. People have wished to make him the first American folk poet. This can only be construed as irony. He lacks the simplicity, the innocence, of the folk poet. The primitiveness of his sensibility lies *anterior* to the people. And his language does not possess quiet strength but noisy power; now and again it rises to loud, orchestral outbursts, exultant shouts of victory that remind the battered reader of Indian war dances. And everywhere, under closer inspection, you find only a wild carnival of words. The author makes prodigious efforts to say something, to convey some meaning in his poems, but he cannot get it out for sheer words. He has poems that consist of practically nothing but names, poems whose individual lines could serve appropriately as poem titles:

Americanos! conquerors! (etc.)
For you a programme of chants.

Chants of the prairies,
Chants of the long-running Mississippi, and down to the
  Mexican sea,
Chants of Ohio, Indiana, Illinois, Iowa, Wisconsin and
  Minnesota,
Chants that run rapidly from the centre of Kansas, and thence
  equidistant (?),
Shooting (forth) in ceaseless pulses of fire to vivify all.[8]

The end! In the next poem he is already talking about something entirely different; for in the next poem he relates how "in ancient times" he sat "studying at the feet of the great masters" but that now in return the old masters "ought to study at his."[9] When you consider that among his old masters he includes first of all Christ, Socrates, and Plato, it is understandable that the civilized reader of the poem finds his own thinking a trifle strained.

It is apparently the long series of names and terms, reeled off in line after line of Whitman's poetry, that has aroused the enthusiasm of Emerson and the English. These inventories, these catalogic columns, are also unquestionably the most unusual and original aspect of his poems. They are literary phenomena. They are without parallel. His entire book is crammed full of these inventories. In a poem of twelve sections, "Song of the Broad-Axe," there is

scarcely a single stanza that does not contain an inventory; one of
these sections is as follows:

> Welcome are all earth's lands, each for its kind,
> Welcome are lands of aspen and oak,
> Welcome are lands of the lemon and fig,
> Welcome are lands of gold,
> Welcome are lands of wheat and maize, welcome those of
>      the grape,
> Welcome are lands of sugar and rice,
> Welcome the cotton-lands, welcome those of the white potato
>      and sweet potato,
> Welcome are mountains, flats, sands, forests, prairies,
> Welcome the rich borders of rivers, table-lands, openings,
> Welcome the measureless grazing-lands, welcome the teeming
>      soil of orchards, flax, honey, hemp;
> Welcome just as much the other more hard-faced lands,
> Lands rich as lands of gold or wheat and fruit lands,
> Lands of mines, lands of the manly (!) and rugged ores,
> Lands of coal, copper, lead, tin, zinc,
> Lands of iron—lands where axes are made.[10]

The ninth section of this same catalogic poem begins with one
of the author's usual incomprehensible parentheses and continues:

> (America! I do not vaunt my love for you,
> I have what I have.)

> The axe leaps!
> The solid forest resounds with fluid utterance,
> They (?) waver, they (?) rise and take form(s),
> Hut, tent, gangplank, survey,
> Flail, plough, pick, crowbar, spade,
> Shingle, bolt, buttress, plank, jamb, lath, panel, gable,
> Citadel, ceiling, saloon, academy, organ, exhibition-house,
>      library,

Cornice, trellis, pilaster, balcony, window, turret, porch,
Hoe, rake, pitchfork, pencil, wagon, staff, saw, jack-plane,
    mallet, wedge, rounce,
Chair, tub, barrel, table, wicket, vane, half-timbering, floor,
Work-box, chest, string'd instrument, boat, frame, and what
    not,
Capitols of States, and capitol of the nation of States,
Long stately rows in avenues, hospitals for orphans or for the
    poor or sick,
Manhattan steamboats and clippers taking the measure of all
    seas.[11]

It is heresy to say so, it is perhaps out-and-out blasphemy, but
I must confess that on dark nights when I have been in great poetic
distress and unable to sleep, I have at times had to clench my teeth
in order not to say straight out: I too could write poems like that!

What does Walt Whitman want? Does he want to abolish the
slave trade in Africa or forbid the use of walking sticks? Does he
want to build a new school house in Wyoming or import woolen
vests for hunters? No one knows. In the art of talking a great deal
and saying absolutely nothing I have never met his match. His
words are ardent; they blaze. There is passion, power, fervor in his
verse. You hear this desperate word-music and you feel his breast
heaving. But you have no idea *why* he is so fervent. Thunder rolls
through his entire book, but the lightning—the spark—never comes.
You read page after page without being able to make sense of anything. You are neither bewildered nor intoxicated by these fervent
tabulations; you are paralyzed, battered to the ground in numb
hopelessness. At last their never-ending, exhausting monotony as-
sails the reader's mind. By the last poem you cannot count to four.
Truly you are confronted with a writer who strains the entire
thought processes of ordinary people. If he but walks on a road
("Song of the Open Road"), he grows rapturous about that road:
"It is worth more to him than a poem," and gradually as he wanders
along this selfsame oft mentioned road, he finds "one divine thing
well envelop'd" after another. He is like a desert dweller who

awakens one morning at an oasis and is overcome with amazement at the sight of grass. "I swear to you," he exclaims, with constant reference to that oft mentioned, much discussed open road, "there are divine things more beautiful than words can tell." And he does not tell either; he does not make the reader any the wiser.

Even with the author's picture vividly before his eyes, the poor reader finds *Leaves of Grass* just as "unspeakably" obscure as the book is without his picture. It is perhaps also highly doubtful that you would understand the poems any better even if you knew the author inside out. At best he could explain personally what he had in mind with his various tabulations. This would not, however, recast them; they are still there right now in a piece of writing that allegedly contains "songs." What Whitman had in mind with his book, though, was *democracy*, according to his own and his biographers' account. He is "the bard of democracy." If he is simultaneously the "bard of the universe," which is what Rhys makes him out to be, then you have to admit that this bard is an extremely versatile man; nor ought you to overlook the fact that from time to time he must have had quite a chore with his tabulations.

Now how is he the "bard of democracy"? In the poem "I Hear America Singing," which contains his manifesto, he is the bard of democracy in the following manner and fashion:

> I hear America singing, the varied carols I hear,
> Those of mechanics, each one singing his as it should
>     be resounding and strong,
> The carpenter singing his as he measures his plank
>     or beam,
> The mason singing his as he makes ready for work, or
>     leaves off work,
> The boatman singing what belongs to him in his boat,
>     the deck-hand singing on the steamboat deck,
> The shoemaker singing as he sits on his bench, the
>     hatter singing as he stands,
> The wood-cutter's song, the ploughboy's on his way in
>     the morning, or at noon intermission or at sundown,

> The delicious singing of the mother, or of the young
>     wife at work, or of the girl sewing or washing,
> Each singing what belongs to him or her and to none
>     else,
> The day what belongs to the day—at night the party
>     of young fellows, robust, friendly,
> Singing with open mouths their strong melodious
>     songs.

He forgets in this poem whose meter beareth all things, endureth all things, and whose lines are without bounds, he forgets to hear the singing of the saddlemakers and the streetcar conductors and the general superintendents. If one of our native bards of democracy composed such a poem, whether it now was about "the shoemaker singing as he sits on his bench" or "the hatter singing as he stands," and he took it to a newspaper or even to a Danish editor of almanacs, I am pretty well convinced that someone would ask to feel the bard's pulse and perhaps offer him a glass of water. If he denied that he was out of his mind, people would in any case think that he carried his jesting to considerable lengths.

Walt Whitman is an American who is moved lyrically; as such he is a rare phenomenon. He has read little or nothing and experienced less than nothing. Extremely few things have happened to him in his lifetime. He was born in 1819; in his twenties he was cheated by his fiancée; during the Civil War he was a nurse; in 1868 he was dismissed from his post in the Department of the Interior and later reinstated; in 1873 his mother died and simultaneously, according to his own statement, something died within him. This is the outline of his life's adventures. Besides *Leaves of Grass* he has written and published a few things, among them, *Specimen Days and Collect* and *Democratic Vistas*, which have, however, in no way consolidated his position in the history of literature. When Whitman's name is mentioned, it is in connection with *Leaves of Grass;* his essays are not read and are in part unreadable.

Had he been born in a highly civilized land and raised intelligently, he might have become a little Wagner; he is sensitive and he has a musical temperament. But having been born in America, that remote corner of the earth where everything bellows hurrah and where the people's only acknowledged talent is selling, he had to remain a changeling, something between primitive being and modern man. "There is in our country," says the American author Nathaniel Hawthorne, "no shadow, no peace, no mysteries, no ideality, no antiquity; but poetry and ivy, wall plants and rambling roses need ruins in order to thrive."[12] In addition to the inborn, natural primitiveness in Whitman's makeup, there is his propensity for more or less primitive reading material; reading the Bible is thus his greatest source of aesthetic pleasure. This has undoubtedly fostered rather than checked his primitive tendencies. Both the accents of the Bible and its mode of thought recur throughout his poetry; in places the similarity between his writing and the Bible is so striking that you almost have to admire the dedication with which he has managed to master such a remote poetic form. Thus in the poem "Song of the Answerer" he says:

> A young man came to me bearing a message from
>     his brother,
> How shall a young man know the whether or
>     when (?) of a brother?
> Tell him to send me the signs.
>
> And I stand before the young man face to face,
>     and take his right hand in my left hand and
>     his left hand in my right hand,
> And I answer for his brother and for men, and I
>     answer for him that answers for all, and I send
>     these signs . . . . .[13]

Does that not read like an excerpt from one of the Old Testament writers? Whitman's daily study of biblical poetry has quite certainly also intensified his literary boldness so that he mentions daring things daringly. He is modern insofar as his pen brutally records all that a fiery sensuality perceives and an uncouth mind thinks. But his realism hardly springs from any conscious sense of artistic courage and responsibility; it is far more the product of that clumsy naiveté which characterizes a child of nature. In reality that section of erotica in *Leaves of Grass* for which he was dismissed from his job and about which an ultra-respectable Boston cried to high heaven contains no more than can be said in all literatures without reproach. It is another thing that his boldness is somewhat crudely, uncouthly expressed, as perhaps it is. With somewhat less naiveté and a little less biblical influence you could say twice as much and also greatly enhance the literary value of what was said—just with a smidgeon of literary dexterity, by shifting a word here, retouching another, by deleting a vulgarity and substituting a precise term. The diction in Whitman's poetry is by no means the most daring, the most ardent, in all literatures, but it is the most tasteless, the most naive in many.

Walt Whitman's naiveté is so disproportionately great that it now and again can even seduce the reader into accepting it. It is this marvelous naiveté of his that has won him a couple of followers even among men of letters. His tabular poetry, those impossible inventories of people, states, housewares, tools, and articles of clothing, is surely the most naive versifying that has ever augmented any literature; and were it not sung by a naive soul, it would assuredly never be read. For it does not show a spark of poetic talent. When Whitman celebrates a thing, he says immediately in the first line that he is celebrating this thing—then he goes ahead in the next line and says he is celebrating a second thing, and in a third line a third—without celebrating it in any other way than by simply naming it. He knows no more about the thing than its name, but he knows many names—whence all his enthusiastic inventories of names. His mind is too restless and his thinking too undisciplined to stick to the simplest thing he sees and to celebrate it; he depicts life in review, not the subtle variations in a particular thing but everything's noisy multiplicity; he always sees en masse. Open his book wherever you like; examine each page—everywhere he says that he wants to sing about this thing or that, but when you come right down to it he still just names it. Interesting in this connection is his little three-line poem entitled "A Farm Picture." Here, because of the nature of his

subject, he had to describe, to picture, something and he does so
then as follows:

> Through the ample open door of the peaceful country
>     barn,
> A sunlit pasture field with cattle and horses feeding,
> And haze and vista, and the far horizon fading away.

The end! This is his farm picture. Barn, countryside, pasture,
cattle, horses, haze, vista, horizon. That the door is ample and the
barn admirably peaceful, that the countryside is sunlit at the same
time that there is a haze, and a haze at the same time that there is a
vista, and these together with the fact, finally, that the horizon is
fading away to hell and gone is really a "description" that with the
years *can* escape the reader's memory! Whitman's unbelievable
naiveté has lured him into putting this poetry into print; his naiveté
even misleads him into believing that he is presenting here a new
kind of literature that is badly needed; in many of his poems he
returns to this idea. "Shut not your doors to me proud libraries," he
exclaims in one place, "For that which was lacking on all your well-
fill'd shelves, yet needed most, I bring."[14] He does not for an instant
doubt his special mission as a writer.

Still, the naiveté of this good man is so fresh and appealing, so
genuine and natural for the wild man, that it never gives the impression of conceit. Even in places where it is most blatantly expressed
and least motivated you do not have the feeling that you are confronted by a vain person. This man is a *good* human being; you feel
as if he had his arm around you as he chants his houseware texts.
In the poem "By Blue Ontario's Shore" he proposes to chant a poem
"that comes from the soul of America," which at the same time is to
be a "carol of victory," as well as a song "of the throes of Democracy."
After having struggled with this rather complex task through fourteen ponderous verses, after having for the ninety-ninth time ran-
sacked "Missouri, Nebraska, and Kansas" and thereafter "Chicago,
Kanada, and Arkansas," he suddenly rears up and stops short. He has
finally reached a conclusion. He dips his pen and writes as follows:

> I swear I begin to see the meaning of these things,
> It is not the earth, it is not America who is so great,
> It is I who am great or to be great . . .

At last he says frankly that America is himself:

> America isolated yet embodying all, what is it
>     finally except myself?
> These States, what are they except myself?

And even here he does not convey any impression of arrogant conceit; it is just naiveté, the staggering naiveté of a wild man.

The best poems in the book are to be found among those Whitman has put together under the common title "Calamus." Here, in singing of *love for humanity,* he strikes chords within his good and warmhearted self which now and again find an echo in others. Through "love of comrades" he wants to renew his corrupted American democracy; by this he will "make the continent indissoluble," "build cities with their arms about each other's necks," "make the most splendid race the sun ever shone upon," "plant comradeship thick as trees along all the rivers," "make divine magnetic lands."[15] Now and again there are wine-filled words in these poems; as such they emerge as rare exceptions in his book. His primitively unrestrained emotional life is expressed here in relatively civilized English so that it is also intelligible to his countrymen. In a poem entitled "Sometimes with One I Love" he is even so conspicuously lucid that in amazement one imagines these two or three lines to have been written by his mother or some other person with sense:

> Sometimes with one I love I fill myself with rage
>     for fear I effuse unreturn'd love,
> But now I think there is no unreturn'd love, the
>     pay is certain one way or another,
> (I loved a certain person ardently and my love
>     was not return'd,
> Yet out of that I have written these songs.)

After all, here we encounter—if among other things we overlook the author's inconsistency of tense between the first and last lines—a lucid thought expressed in readable language—a language, true enough, which when considered for its lyrical qualities is somewhat juridical. But he cannot contain himself for long; a few verses farther on he is again the incomprehensible primitive. In one poem he suggests in all seriousness that he is personally there with every single reader of his book: "Be not too certain but I am now with you," he warns.[16] In the next poem he grows highly dubious about Walt Whitman's shadow:

> My shadow . . .
> How often I find myself standing and looking at it
>     where it flits,
> How often I question and doubt whether that is
>     really me! . . . .[17]

It occurs to me that this doubt is not totally unwarranted, considering that one is endowed with a shadow that has the knack of flitting about while the individual himself stands still and observes it.

Whitman is one of those naturally gifted, highly responsive human beings who are born too late. In "Song of the Open Road" he reveals perhaps most clearly what a kindhearted, sweet disposition he has, together with the pervasive naiveté in his ideas. If these verses had been composed in a slightly more reasonable manner, more of them would be poetry; such is not the case now, when the author constantly frustrates an understanding of his poems with the massive verbal apparatus he employs. He cannot say a thing simply and tellingly; he is unable to *describe* anything precisely. He says a thing five times, always in the same grand but imprecise manner. He does not control his material; he lets the material control him. It manifests itself for him in colossal forms; it piles up and overwhelms him. In all these poems of the open road his heart is warmer than his head is cool; he can therefore neither depict nor celebrate; he can only shout with joy—shout at the top of his lungs with joy over everything and nothing. You can feel the powerful beating of a heart in these pages, but you search in vain for a reasonable explanation for this heart's having been so intensely moved. That a mere open road as such can make a heart pound is incomprehensible. It intoxicates Whitman; he says so frankly, his breast throbbing with ecstasy: "I could stop here and do miracles." How his good and joyous heart leads him astray! "I think whatever I shall meet on the road I shall like," he sings, "and whoever beholds me shall like me, I think whoever sees me shall be happy." He adds in his strange, inaccurate language: "Whoever denies me it shall not trouble me,/ Whoever accepts me he or she shall be blessed and shall bless me."[18] He is earnest, earnest and good. At times even he himself is so amazed by his extraordinary goodness that this naive soul goes ahead and sings: "I am larger, better than I thought, I did not know I held so much goodness."

He is more a rich human being than a talented poet. Walt Whitman cannot write, of course. But he can feel. He lives a life of mood and emotion. If he had not received that letter from Emerson, his book would have fallen silently into oblivion—which it deserved to do.

Ralph Waldo Emerson is America's most significant thinker, finest aesthetician, and most distinctive man of letters; this is not, however, the same as being the most distinguished thinker, aesthetician, and man of letters in one of the great European countries. For many years—through half his lifetime—he was his country's arbiter of literary taste, and certainly no one was better suited to this than he; he was a meticulously educated man—he was well-read, had traveled some and seen the world outside America. He was not a universal intellect and he was not a genius; he was a talented man whose greatest, most highly developed talent was his very intelligent understanding. He had the gift of captivating others. He was able to charm people not only with his polished diction but also nearly always with his appealing treatment of topics which, it is true, were usually chosen on the basis of his own likes; he did not manage to do so with either his originality or his brilliance. When he had seen or heard something, he was just enough taken with the thing to write about it and write well. All the topics he discusses are precisely those that could affect just such a nature as Emerson's.

The intellectual currents of three continents converged in this man—the mystical, the aesthetic, and the practical. From Asia he got his religious bent; from Europe his craving for intelligence, art, and beauty; from his homeland he had that congenital inheritance of democratic narrowmindedness and practical Yankee commonsense. This blend of Eastern and Western cultures shaped his mind and determined his life. From birth he was a Puritan; he belonged to a long line of English ministers; his upbringing was proper and moral; he himself became a minister. Too much influenced by modern thought and situated right in the middle of the world's most wildly pulsating business society, he could not very well espouse all the religious mysticism of Asia without denying his modernity; he accepted therefore only as much as his practical commonsense allowed. On the other hand, he also satisfied all his religious inclinations. He needed a God and he took a God; he had no special need for eternal damnation and he took a transitory hell—in short, he became that unfathomable combination of blind faith and partial radicalism called the Unitarian. His birth, his upbringing, his nature, and his reading made a "liberal" minister of Emerson and a moral man. The God of Christ became his God, Goethe's Mephistopheles his devil, and the sorely platonic Plato his philosopher. To a rare degree he became a person of the past and present. The varying warmth of three different latitudes inhabited his mind; and as the tropical sun is the hottest, so Asia's contribution to Emerson's mind was the dominant one. He became a *religious* man. He was rarely worldly, even more rarely free-spoken, never radical; in whatever he wrote he was religious or at least moral. Thus it is that this gifted American was a minister in a Christian church and wrote philosophical treatises in his spare time. Swedenborg, the Bible, Schelling, and Fichte, but first and last Plato, took up residence in this man's heart, creating a hitherto unknown philosophical formula in America; he became the most comprehensively educated Yankee writer. Since 1882 his grave has been one of America's historical attractions.

His major work is *Representative Men* (1849), a little book, far shorter than this one—"his best book."[19] This book is also the best known, distinguished and elegant in diction, composed in short pieces, lacking in system, full of contradictions, alternately penetrating and superficial, everywhere interesting. Of other works, Emerson has written a variety of articles for papers and magazines, consistently himself throughout, always intelligent, constantly operating partly with morality and partly with aesthetic criticism. His achievement was never greater than in *Representative Men,* but even in his last sermons he stood at about the same level as there. His essays and other writings bear the titles *Infinite God; Cure of Asthma by a Stroke of Lightning; Nature; Poems; On Divining Rod, with References to the Use Made of It in Its Exploring for Springs of Water; The Power Above; Lectures on New England Reformers; English Traits; Tobacco, a Remedy for Arsenic; On Eastern Literature of Old.* As can be seen, the same blend of Eastern mysticism and Western reality—in all these works he is the religiously moral Unitarian and an interesting writer.

Emerson's most significant talent as *critic* is his intelligent understanding, the cultivated and gifted man's ability to grasp a book, an event, an age correctly. He is methodical, on the other hand, only in a very figurative sense. He reads a writer's books, takes pleasure in their beauty, frowns at their defects, jots down the necessary quotations, and puts the books aside. Thereafter he reads the author's biography, marks the most important data, joyfully fastens upon a date with or without significance, and out of curiosity examines the man's private life with a fine-tooth comb. With this background he writes an essay and he writes it well. He always has good things to say; he is interesting, intermittently clever, once a year even witty. But his criticism is not scientific, it is not modern. He rejects and approves, sets up rules, judges one writer against another without carefully taking into account the distinctive qualities of each, and proves on the basis of his pre-established Mount Sinai laws how the work at hand is faulty or malformed both on pages 113 and 209. This is especially true of his literary essays. He is the last little aesthetician representing the tyranny of rules. As Shakespeare constitutes his highest standard in drama, so Plato does in philosophy;

beyond them lies a pathless wilderness. He never stops to consider whether a work might be a fortuitous event, a happenstance, having arisen as a caprice, a mood, without any previous history and without roots; he does not evaluate it on the basis of its own premises any more than his critical impartiality ever tricks him into making his mind up about an author on the basis of the man himself. He looks everything up in his rules and compares. This is his task as critic, and it rests upon a personal view. Emerson himself has explained how criticism, when all is said and done, still means to *measure*. The extent to which he recognizes and acknowledges this tenet can be seen from the following brief and precise statement about Plato: "The way to know him is to compare him, not with nature, but with other men."[20] This statement, among many similar ones, gives an idea of the nature of Emerson's critical judgment.

He is a man of taste. There was no one in America who could captivate a feminine audience as Emerson could in his best days. He offended no one and was interesting to all. His appearance was elegant, his manners distinguished, his voice appealing; his gestures were those of an experienced speaker, rather unobtrusive, a trifle clerical; above all his diction was exquisite. It is neither his profundity nor his knowledge of literature that makes him interesting as a critic. There is curiously little in all he has written that could not have been said by any cultured individual, with but the exception of his remarkable style. No, this man's primary interest lies in the fact that he possessed to a truly unusual degree that happy faculty of a writer or a speaker of being able to *say things*. Tasteful things, interesting things, good things. There are writers, notably among journalists and essayists—I mention at random Rochefort—whose remarkable gift, talent, lies in writing exceedingly well about a topic, making ingenious, inspired statements which do not always have to concern the topic but which nevertheless do not sound abstract because they belong to the *text*, fit the sentence, and give life to the article. Such an article is always read with interest because it is interesting in itself, without its therefore explaining an issue or presenting information or keeping to the title. Without doing Emerson an injustice, it can be said that he has something of this strange gift. His writings teem with these short, exquisite sentences which do not always contain anything about the topic but which contain something in themselves and belong to his production, something extra, something well done—comparisons, allusions, abrupt shifts in thought, a flash, a hint, a word—something that everyone could not say but that everyone finds admirable when it is said. If on the other hand one turns to the *subject,* if one asks what he actually has proved, illuminated, or defined with all his good things, then one is amazed at how extraordinarily little the man has really dealt with a topic during the shorter or longer period he has held our attention. Take an example. *Representative Men* opens with a lecture on "Uses of Great Men." There are tasteful things, interesting things, good things. But what is the substance of this lecture? *That one can learn something from great men.* What a striking truth! But I knew that ten years before I was confirmed. Imagine sitting for an hour to hear that you can learn something from great men. Just think of it, a whole hour! And yet there is no reason to believe that Emerson at the time bored his listeners, any more than that one is bored now in reading his lecture; he has, you see, been interesting; he has said things. He goes so far with this gospel truth, one can learn something from great men, that he establishes without question that "the man simply makes men."[21] True enough, he himself ruins this tenet on page 122 of the same book in an essay on Shakespeare, but it is extremely entertaining to follow his argument, and he has our undivided attention as long as he talks. The man makes men. "Every ship that comes to America got its chart from Columbus. Every novel is a debtor to Homer." "Plato is philosophy, and philosophy Plato." "Out of Plato come all things that are still written and debated among men of thought [. . .] St. Augustine, Copernicus, Newton, Behmen, Swedenborg, Goethe, are all Plato's debtors and say after him." These names enliven a dull moment. In a lecture where such things are said, one never yawns; one learns nothing, one is not convinced, but one listens. One could raise objections. One could cite Plato himself: "Philosophy in all its parts does not meet in one man but springs up in different persons" (*Republic*); one could prove that Plato also had predecessors he was indebted to—

Solon, Sophron, Socrates—but one savors a couple of interesting absurdities in a lecture on philosophy.[22] One accepts such entertainment without a murmur.

This talent of Emerson's for saying good things does not greatly enhance his competence as a critic. There is so little depth and originality in his criticism that it often depends entirely on the exemplary form of its presentation. Emerson cannot infuse a thing with life; he does not become completely familiar with the object to be criticized; he circles around it, alternately falling behind it and passing it by. One reads all his excellent comments; one reads while awaiting a conclusion relevant to the subject itself. One awaits the third and final word that can draw a figure or cast a statue. One waits until the twentieth and final page—one waits in vain: at this point Emerson bows and departs. And the reader is left with a lapful of things said; they have not formed a picture; they are a brilliant welter of small, elegant mosaic tiles.

If I were to attempt to identify Emerson's major failings as a critic, I would first of all mention his undeveloped *psychological* sense and thereafter his overdeveloped *moral* sense. His conception of a book or person is much too schematic. He has no eye for the slight stirrings of the psyche, the delicate manifestations of will and instinct, all that subtle life of nameless shadings; he understands a given action correctly and intelligently but not the inception of that action. He glides around a book drawing threads out of it, without perceiving that the book is a fabric. (See, *inter alia,* his commentary on *Wilhelm Meister.*) He acts the same way with a writer; he sees him in fragments, fleetingly, collaring him in an act, falling upon him at a date, and before and after leaving him in peace. Because of this lack of psychological insight in Emerson's criticism, one never finds the vibrant word, that stroke of the pen that brings a figure to life. The *life* of the subject has not been imparted to him, and he of course is unable to impart it to others. Emerson's grasp of psychology, even in his treatment of Plato, whose being he has penetrated most deeply, is exceedingly superficial; the treatment became a eulogy, a panegyric, but not a characterization. You do not interpret a writer by saying admirable things in connection with his name and filling an essay with an elegant but chaotic mosaic of words—that is not the man, the person.

But if Emerson thus lacks even the most essential knowledge of psychology, he has in recompense an excess of the moral sentiment. He is a Puritan, he is an Asiatic, a fetishist. From the worship of an orthodox fetish he turned to the worship of a modernized one, but like the Muslim he continued until his death to turn his eyes to the East when he knelt. Morality was and remained his basic instinct; it was inborn; it had been poured into his blood through several generations. Emerson's forebears were ministers for all of eight consecutive generations, and even he declares with a pride that arouses one's compassion that he "smacks of the soil."[23] Nor in truth do you read very much of Emerson's production before perceiving how rankly he smacks of the soil. In his criticism this man, whom a large nation was obliged to have as literary arbiter and chief for forty years, acts like someone who is a special spokesman for the Lord, like a censorious man of God who impales sin on a spit and holds it up as a warning and a lesson, like a midget Goliath armed with a splinter from the jawbone of a biblical ass, with which he gesticulates: no sin, no vice, no guilt, no human going astray so long as my name is Ralph Waldo Emerson! Morality has softened the brain of this excellent man and impaired his critical sense. He feels sorry for Voltaire because he said of "the good Jesus," "Let me never hear that man's name again,"[24] he invokes and quotes the Veda, Bhagavad Gita, Akhlak-y-Jalaly, Vishnu Purana, Krishna, Yoganidra, the Koran, and the Bible in aesthetic and philosophical definitions; he regrets Shakespeare's frivolous life with a pastoral piety that does honor to all straitlaced rightmindedness. This man, who condemns all that is base and ridiculous and enthusiastically applauds all that is fine and good in life, has through half a lifetime led literature in a country like America where people live such sinfully immoral lives and where no one—outside of Boston—gives a hoot about the Christian virtues. Emerson might fairly be compared with England's John Ruskin, with whom morally he has most in common, although

Ruskin's knowledge of aesthetics, to be sure, far exceeds his own. Just like Ruskin he operates with moral prescriptions in his criticism; he is lavish with opinions that are universally respectable; and he demonstrates with Plato in hand and condemns with the Bible in his heart. Taken as a whole, his magazine articles constitute the most respectable and unadulterated defense for a divine aesthetic on earth. He is critic and cleric, and cleric as critic. He dares not say about Goethe—well, let me quote him. What Emerson dares not say about Goethe is characteristic of a critic:

"I dare not say that Goethe ascended to the highest grounds from which genius has spoken. He has not worshiped the highest unity; he is impregnable as a fortress for moral sentiments. There are nobler efforts in poetry than any he has contributed to it. There are writers poorer in talent, whose tone is purer, and more touches the heart. Goethe can never be dear to men. His is not even the devotion to pure truth; but truth for the sake of cultural progress. He has no aims less large than the conquest of universal nature, of universal truth" (*On Goethe: A Lecture*).[25] What immorality! How sinful! Emerson is not saying this in jest at all; that man's total lack of irony is the highest "pure truth" I know.

If you would now like to know how he deals critically with Shakespeare, then begin reading *Representative Men* on page 115. Shakespeare is—to begin with—"the best dramatist in the world." Thereafter Shakespeare's "mind is the horizon beyond which we still cannot see"; "his works seem to have fallen down to him from heaven"; he has written "the airs for all [. . .] modern music"; "his means are as admirable as his ends"; "for executive faculty, for creation, Shakespeare is unique"; our "literature, philosophy and thought are Shakespearized." Taine's panegyric to Shakespeare is criticism in comparison to this. Citing an English writer, Emerson now demonstrates Shakespeare's marvelous knack of stealing both ideas and text from everywhere for his dramas; he makes the rather daring assertion, moreover, that "assuredly none of Shakespeare's dramas is his own invention." He cites the fact that of 6,043 lines in *Henry VI*, 1,771 lines were written by someone else, 2,373 were written by someone else but rewritten by Shakespeare, and finally only 1,899 were written by Shakespeare himself. Now how does Emerson get this information to jibe with Shakespeare's "unique creation," with his "admirable means," and with his own *saying* that Shakespeare's works "have fallen down to him from heaven"? Yes, indeed, says Emerson—"all originality is relative," says he; "every thinker is retrospective." "It is easy to see," he goes on to say, "that what is best written or done by genius in the world is not one man's work, but is wrought by the labors of thousands." What does that now do to his Plato? And, of course, the man making men? He thinks about this relative originality for a while, and then he continues: "The learned member of the legislature, at Westminster or at Washington, speaks and votes for thousands." Which is an example of how all originality is relative and every thinker retrospective! He does not, however, leave it at that; he has additional proofs. Now the Asiatic rears up in him; the Fetish appears before his eyes, the critic disappears and the cleric remains. For on the same page of a *literary* study where he catches an author stealing, he gets a chance to give the following information—about the *Bible:* "Our English Bible is a wonderful specimen of the strength and music of the English language. But it was not made by one man, or at one time; but centuries and churches brought it to perfection. There has never been a time when one or another translation has not been in progress. Our Liturgy, admired for its energy and pathos, is an anthology of the piety of ages and nations, a translation of the prayers and forms of the Catholic church—these collected, too, in long periods, from the prayers and meditations of every saint and pious writer all over the world." To this Emerson appends a statement by Grotius, who remarks in respect to the Lord's Prayer that even this had long been in use among the rabbis before Christ came and "collected" it.[26]

Why does Emerson offer this information in this connection? In order to explain what goes on with these retrospective thinkers, in order to demonstrate the absolute relativity of originality as well as, finally and at last, to show what a basically innocent thing it was for Shakespeare to steal ideas and text from others for his works. If it is done in the Bible, then others can do it; Emerson does not have one word to say against it. Now the fact is, however, that for such gross literary dishonesty as Shakespeare's the criminal code of today would hopefully mete out a severe rap on the fingers as well as cause trouble for an editor of the Lord's Prayer. That is how much more civilized Goethe's "truth for the sake of cultural progress" is than Emerson's "pure" truth. It would be far easier for every author to sit down and compose as Shakespeare did than to try to do everything himself. If one nowadays could help oneself freely to the language and ideas in, for example, Goethe's work and if one could use this material on the same broad scale as did Shakespeare, then even one of Walt Whitman's "hatmakers" could turn out a couple of *Fausts* per year—this does not mean, however, that in so doing he could hold a candle to Shakespeare as a poet.

Our moral Emerson does not have a single word of censure for the slightly outdated manner in which Shakespeare handles the literary property of others; on the contrary, he explains it philosophically by saying that all originality is relative and morally by saying that the same thing has gone on in the Bible. What Emerson finds cause to criticize, on the other hand, is Shakespeare's somewhat disreputable personal life, his *life as a man.* Here Emerson again reveals the range and nature of his critical ability, the meagerness of his psychological understanding. What concern is it to a critic how a writer spends his days and nights, except insofar as this life has left its mark on the man's work? The question then is: Did Shakespeare's frivolous life damage his writing? Diminish his works? Dull his sensibilities? Thwart his productiveness? The question is more than superfluous. Shakespeare gained a knowledge in precisely those areas barred by the aesthetics of Emerson and the rest of Boston which is so impressive, so intense and penetrating, that he is today still regarded as a fully qualified analyst of the mind to whom no passion, no sin, or desire of any kind was foreign. And this intimate knowledge of human vice and error, without which the value of his writings would surely have been significantly reduced and his art to the same extent limited—this knowledge was in fact gained by Shakespeare's having lived as he did, by giving himself over to the diversity of life and thus learning by experience the entire range, not so often of a feeling, but more frequently of a passion or frenzy. Emerson does not even have half an eye for this fact. He does not say a word about the necessity, not even the usefulness, of Shakespeare's personal experience with living; his psychological understanding does not reach any further than to the least human aspect of man, that is, morality. He is pure virtuousness. He deplores that Shakespeare lived a sinful life, and his complaint rests upon morality. "The Shakespeare Society has brought to light," he says, "that Shakespeare took part in and provided lively entertainment. I can find no pleasure in this demeaning fact. Other admirable men have led lives in some sort of keeping with their thought; but this man, in wide contrast. Had he been less, had he reached only the common measure of great authors, of Bacon, Milton, Tasso, Cervantes, we could surrender his life to the twilight of human fate: but this man of men, he who gave to human thought a new and larger foundation than had ever existed, and planted the standards of humanity all the way into Chaos—that he should not be wise for himself!—it must even go into the world's history that the best poet led a low and unholy life, using his genius for the public amusement" (*Representative Men*).[27]

Note this speech; it is very characteristic of Emerson's reasoning and style of writing. Innumerable passages resemble this one. Every one of his pages contains these artful, interesting nonsensicalities. In the first place he cannot find pleasure in Shakespeare's being "lusty"; not if his life depended on it can Emerson find pleasure in this; for him it is a "demeaning fact" about this same Shakespeare. Thereafter he comes with the remarkable statement—in the same book in which he treats Napoleon and Goethe!—that other men have lived in some sort of keeping with their "thought" but not Shakespeare—unfortunately. If it had read *teachings* instead of thought, the sentence as such would at any rate be logical; as it now stands, it is nonsense. Perhaps Shakespeare was not so completely *unthinking* in his frivolity; his sonnets, among other things, show that he meditated about his excesses in some detail. And can one ever—not just once but throughout an entire lifetime—lead a frivolous life without one's mind having thought, having willed, that existence? If it is a question, however, of living according to one's *teachings,* then Shakespeare's fate here is no different from that of many admirable men, despite Emerson's apparent lack of suspicion. It is hard to have to live according to one's teachings! It was even hard for Emerson's own "good Jesus," who, while teaching love and tolerance, reviled intelligent men and heaped abuse upon them— men whose knowledge and range of ability were greater than Jesus' ability to tally them up. Emerson ought to know that it is hard to live according to one's teachings! What else does he have against Shakespeare's life? He does not find fault with him because he had that idiosyncrasy of appropriating what belonged to others; on the other hand he is dissatisfied with him because he was "lusty." On page 126 of the same treatise, however, he cites the "fact" that Shakespeare was "in all respects a good husband." Wherein was he then "lusty"? Finally, having demonstrated Shakespeare's thievish habits at great length, Emerson still calls him the "best poet"; not satisfied with this, he takes an even bigger bite in regard to Shakespeare the man. Emerson shows little consideration in either his admiration or his disapproval; he overdoes them—he jumps the track. He admires Shakespeare, he celebrates Shakespeare, he even makes him a *man of men*—in the same breath that he very profoundly disapproves of precisely the "low, unholy life" of Shakespeare the man. Add to this that he says here that Shakespeare "used his genius for the public amusement" in a *depreciatory* sense—after having extolled him as the "subtlest of authors," whose works are creations "which seem to have fallen down to him from heaven."

This is that vacillating posture that characterizes Emerson's talent for *saying things*. His criticism is a little too irrelevant for me, a little too facile; that kind of criticism is based entirely on an acquired education rather than on an unusually well-endowed natural talent. Emerson's strength is understanding rooted in morality. His criticism is rhetorical, and his critical talent is therefore essentially literary. He can write an essay about anything; he can select a topic like "Infinite God" or pretty much its opposite like "Tobacco, a Remedy for Arsenic"—his considerable literary talent is set in motion, and he is just as interesting discussing mystical things as real things. Emerson's talent for writing an article under a heading, his flair for saying things, is no secret to him. In numerous places in his treatises he admits having this gift, and he recognizes it as the writer's most important talent. Thus he says of Shakespeare (*Representative Men*): "Shakespeare's principal merit may be summarized in saying that he of all men best understood the English language, and could say what he would."[28] Of Emerson one can say: He understood the English language and could say what he would; even in a treatise he could say things that were irrelevant to the *topic,* which he, precisely by dint of his literary talent, nevertheless knew how to make relevant to the *treatise* as a finished product. In a philosophical lecture on Plato he gives us five minutes of literary entertainment about Socrates. He does it well, with style, vividly. He has all our attention and we again listen:

> Socrates, a man of humble stem, but honest enough; of the commonest history; of a personal ugliness so great that since then it has become a witticism . . . The players caricatured him on the stage; the potters copied his ugly head on their stone jugs. He was a cold fellow who united humor with the most complete self-control. In addition there was his knowledge of human nature. He always saw through his man, laying him bare in every debate—and in debate he was immoderately entertaining. The young men are prodigiously fond of him and invite him to their feasts, whither he goes for conversation. He can drink, too; has the strongest head in Athens; and after leaving the whole party under the table, goes away as if nothing had happened, to begin new dialogues with somebody that is sober. In short, he was what our country people call *an old one.*
>
> He [. . .] was monstrously fond of Athens, hated trees, never willingly went beyond the walls, knew the old titles, knew how to distinguish between people and philistines, thought every thing in Athens a little better than anything in any other place. He was plain as a Quaker in habit and speech, and used phrases and illustrations from the lowest walks of life, from soup-pans to unnamable conveniences—especially if he talked with any superfine person. He had a Franklin-like wisdom. Thus he showed one who was afraid to go on foot all the way to Olympia, that the stretch was no more than Socrates' daily walks within doors.

Plain old uncle [. . .] he was, with his great ears, an immense talker . . . He is very poor; but then he is hardy as a soldier, and can live on a few olives, usually [. . .] on bread and water, except when entertained by his friends. His necessary expenses were exceedingly small, and no one could live as he did. He wore no under garment; his upper garment was the same for summer and winter, and he always went barefooted; and it is said that to satisfy his desire to talk all day with [. . .] cultivated young men, he will now and then return to his shop and carve statues, good or bad, for sale. However that be, it is certain that he had grown to delight in nothing else than this conversation; and that, under his [. . .] pretense of knowing nothing, he attacks and brings down all the fine speakers, all the fine philosophers of Athens [. . .] Nobody can refuse to talk with him, he is so honest and really curious to know everything; a man who was willingly confuted if he did not speak the truth, and who willingly confuted others asserting what was false; and not less pleased when confuted than when confuting [. . .] A pitiless disputant, who knows nothing, but whose unconquerable intelligence no man has ever reached; whose temper was imperturbable; whose dreadful logic was always leisurely and sportively at work; so careless and ignorant as to disarm the wariest and draw them, in the most polite manner into horrible doubts and confusion. But he always knew the way out; knew it, yet would not tell it. No escape; he drives them to terrible choices [. . .] and tosses the Hippiases and Gorgiases [. . .] as a boy tosses his balls. The tyrannous realist! —Meno has debated more than a thousand times and done very well, as it appeared to him; but at this moment he cannot say anything—this cramp-fish of a Socrates has so bewitched him (*Representative Men*).[29]

All very interesting, splendid, literary but without critical analysis and totally without depth. A character sketch of the real Socrates would have to be different; it would have to have a *soul*. Aside from the fact that Emerson here is using Socrates primarily as a measure of Socrates' own pupil Plato, whom he worships and therefore about whom he cannot be totally detached, there is nothing in this sketch that gets at the heart of the man—the philosopher. He does not so much as mention a word about his philosophical teachings, either the nature of his positive philosophy or its fundamentally ethical character; he presents him as that "ignorant intellect,"[30] street debater, windbag, idler. There were so many "ignorant intellects" on the streets of Athens in the fourth century B.C.—why are their names not two thousand years old as well? And why is Socrates'? The fact is, Emerson simply cannot get at the core of the object under analysis. He lacks the psychological prerequisites: that is, a penetrating, discerning eye and a throbbing, acutely sensitive sympathy that perceives everything. He always seizes upon the object only for the moment and discovers in it what any other highly cultivated individual is able to find there, but no more. Otherwise his precedence as critic over any other cultivated individual turns upon talents of a purely literary nature.

He presents Napoleon as "the man of the world." "He is no hero, in the high sense. The man in the street finds in him the qualities and powers of other men in the street [. . .] Sociability, good books, fast travelling, dress, dinners, servants without number, personal weight, the ability to realize one's ideas, the standing in the attitude of a benefactor to all persons about him, the refined enjoyments of pictures, statutes, music, palaces and conventional honors—absolutely everything that is dear to the heart of every man in the nineteenth century, this powerful man possessed." Napoleon "was the idol of common men because he had in transcendent degree the qualities and powers of common men." "With him is no miracle and no magic. He is a worker in brass, in iron, in wood, in earth, in roads, in buildings, in money and in troops, and a very consistent and wise foreman." "He is brave, sure, self-denying, self-neglecting, sacrificing every thing—money, troops, generals [. . .] for the sake of the cause; not misled, like common adventurers, by the splendor of his great deeds."[31]

A couple of pages farther on he draws up a more complete character sketch of this same Napoleon—a sketch that is in part different from the first, in part self-contradictory:

Bonaparte was singularly destitute of generous sentiments. The highest-placed individual in the most cultivated age and population of the world—he has not the merit of common truth and honesty. He is unjust to his generals; egotistic and monopolizing; [. . .] stealing the credit of their great actions from Kellermann, from Bernadotte . . . He is a boundless liar. The official paper, his "Moniteur," and all his bulletins, are only filled with things that he wished to be believed; and worse—he sat, in his premature old age, in his lonely island, coldly falsifying facts and dates and figures . . . He was thoroughly unscrupulous. He would steal, slander, assassinate, drown and poison, as his interest dictated. He had no generosity, but mere vulgar hatred; he was intensely selfish; he was perfidious; he cheated at cards; he was a prodigious gossip, and opened letters [. . .] and rubbed his hands with joy when he had intercepted some secret morsel concerning the men and women about him, boasting that "he knew every thing"; and interfered with the cutting of the dresses of the women; and listened after the hurrahs and the compliments of the street, incognito. His manners were coarse; he treated women with low familiarity. He had the habit of pulling their ears and pinching their cheeks when he was in good humor, and of pulling the ears and whiskers of men . . . It does not appear that he listened at keyholes, or at least that he was caught at it. In short, when you have penetrated through all the circles of power and splendor, you were not dealing with a gentleman, at last.[32]

But the mistakes "that finally made the people turn away from him were not Bonaparte's fault," Emerson goes on to say. "He did all that in him lay [. . .]—*without moral principle.*"[33]

And there we have it!

In considering Emerson as a *philosopher*, it must be borne in mind that the man is a Unitarian. The fundamental principles of the Christian lie at the root of his thinking: man, sin, punishment, God. Just as he is a moralist as critic, he is a Unitarian as philosopher. The Unitarian religion allows just that much latitude for philosophic speculation as is tolerable to a "liberally" oriented worshiper of God; on the other hand, it is a protection against all foolhardy metaphysical radicalism. The Unitarian religion operates halfway between knowledge and faith—it is wise like a serpent, innocent like a dove, here snapping up an apple of knowledge from the Eden of this world, there following attentively every head-shaking prohibition of the great Fetish. What the Unitarian philosophy is unable to make out through speculative means, it sets five men to *believe* in, and that point which all the positivists in the world still have not reached in thousands of years—that is, the final synthesis and conclusion—the Unitarian philosophy of faith reaches in less time than it takes to think. A comfortable and relatively facile philosophy, a haven in life and death, a consolation, a resting place, a delight for the tired human mind, a mode of speculation that has its strength precisely in its weakness: that is, the least reflection possible.

Emerson is a Unitarian. His philosophy is half philosophic thought and half faith—there is no uncertainty, no searching, but right from the start a finished philosophic system. Observations, comparisons, experiments, hypotheses—all the inductive methods of speculation—hold virtually no interest for him: "Philosophy is Plato." (Cf. *Fortnightly Review*, IX, 1883.[34]) This man, who has founded no school, who has established no system, who has not thought a single new thought, who has not even *adopted* a single new thought, who has never, never written an original work—this man is America's sole philosopher. In encyclopedias and lexicons he is entered as follows: "Emerson, R. W., North American poet and philosopher. Writings: *Representative Men*."

How does it happen that Emerson's name has even been mentioned in connection with philosophic thought? In the first place because he is the only one who represents philosophic training in all of Yankeeland. In the second place because he really has the qualifications for ingratiating himself with a public: he has considerable literary talent—he can write. He has that felicitous gift of the essayist and he uses it with tact. He can compose the most charming paradoxes in an elegant and properly learned philosophic language; he is a master at creating good, polished sentences, at working in mosaic. During a deadly calm he surprises us with a sentence that whips like a silken banner in the wind; he keeps us wide awake with the most elegant self-contradictions, astonishing us with a bold assertion, challenging our sense of logic without blinking an eye. But a thinker, no, that he is not. He is too superficial, too feminine. Emerson himself admits this in a treatise: "I delight in telling what I think, but if you ask me how I dare say so, or why it is so, I am the most helpless of mortal men."[35] However, in a philosophy that so strongly emphasizes the absolute relativity of originality, as does Emerson's, there is only a very modest need for causes and proofs.

What is Emerson's philosophy?

"Philosophy is the account which the human mind gives to itself of the constitution of the world. Two cardinal facts lie [. . .] at the base [. . .]—1. Unity, or Identity; and, 2. Plurality, or Variety" (*Representative Men*). Fine! Philosophy then is something that on the one hand is one thing and on the directly opposite hand is the directly opposite thing. Why not? We are used to a little of everything from men of philosophy. "We unite all things by perceiving the law which pervades them," Emerson continues with a certain scholarly obscurity, "by perceiving the superficial differences and the profound resemblances. But every mental act—this very perception of identity or oneness, recognizes the diversity of things [. . .] It is impossible to speak or to think without embracing both. The mind is inclined to ask for one cause of many effects . . . a fundamental unity." And here Emerson suddenly cites the Vedas: "In the midst of the sun is the light, in the midst of the light is truth, and in the midst of truth is *the imperishable being*."[36]

Now you should agree that if there is one thing in the world the Unitarian hates, it is this: not to be able to find the final synthesis and arrive at the ultimate conclusion. Emerson uses half an octavo page to resolve the mystery of whether or not there is an "imperishable being," and he takes it for granted that there is; he is not afraid to say that there is; he establishes definitively that there is a God. One might be tempted to ask him if he had it in writing.

Now Emerson goes on for a whole three and a half lines to develop how the two cardinal elements that occur in philosophy—the positive and the subjective, which he identifies more specifically as effect (the world) and cause (God)—are mutually contradictory. "The tendency of the first of these cardinal elements is escape from organization (!)—pure science; and the tendency of the other is the highest serviceableness, or use of means, or executive deity."[37]

After this definition—a definition that strikes me as being a bit top-heavy—Emerson tosses out one of those terse, lucid things he *says* that reveals in a flash how thoroughly Unitarian the workings of his mind are, how firmly he is planted halfway between philosophic thought and faith: "Each thinker adheres, by temperament and by habit, to the first or to the second of these gods of the mind. By religion, he tends to unity; by intellect, or by the senses, to the many. A too rapid unification, and an excessive appliance to parts and particulars, are the twin dangers of speculation."[38]

There that man hangs, dangling between heaven and earth, and he feels so extraordinarily comfortable that he cries out that the danger lies in *not* dangling between heaven and earth. Go forth and do thou likewise!

Now once again, what is Emerson's philosophy? Emerson's philosophy is *Plato*.

For him Plato is history's greatest thinker. "Plato is philosophy, and philosophy, Plato." "Be another: not thyself, but a Platonist." "Plato's fame does not stand on a syllogism, or on any masterpieces of the Socratic reasoning, or on any thesis, as for example the immortality of the soul. He is more than a man of experience, or a schoolman, or a geometer, or the prophet of a peculiar message. He represents the privilege of the intellect, of the power of mind. He has carried all facts to logical, successive stages and disclosed in each fact a germ of truth that encompasses all of space. Everywhere he takes roads that have no end, but run continuously round the entire universe." Among those "facts," then, which Plato "has carried to logical, successive stages," Emerson mentions his doctrine on the immortality of the soul and adds: "What comes from God to us, returns from us to God." He loves Plato because Plato has such a great need for a God. "The soul in man is the divine element liberated and detached from nature. Body cannot teach one wisdom—God only." He admires Plato because even in antiquity Plato had

found that "poetry, prophecy and profound visions are from a
wisdom of which man is not master." And last, he worships Plato
for exactly the same reason that he loves and admires him—he is the
greatest of God worshipers: Plato "stands between the truth and
every man's mind." "He has penetrated into worlds which people
of flesh and blood cannot reach; he saw the souls in pain, he hears
the doom of the judge." "I am struck [. . .] with the extreme
modernness of his style and spirit. Here is the germ of that Europe
we know so well, in its long history of arts and arms; here are all its
stages mapped out beforehand in the mind of Plato—and by none
before him. Europe has since split into hundreds of histories, but
has added no new element to Plato's European history. Plato became
Europe, and philosophy, and almost literature." "One can cite proofs
for both sides of every great question from Plato."[39]

Examine these statements a bit; they are again characteristic of
Emerson's remarkable talent for saying things. The exaggeration
about Plato's being Europe, philosophy, and literature is not important and ought to be overlooked; it is an *American* exaggeration,
of value only as a specimen of good Yankee style. It is useful therefore instead to examine the value and logical content of these various theses.

Emerson is enthralled with Plato because he is the *infallible*
thinker. Even Europe has had to fulfill his prophecies and not de-
viate from them with any "new element." Now since Plato "stands
between the truth and every man's mind," every man has to go
either past or through Plato to find the truth. One comes then to
this truthful Plato but discovers that in him there are "proofs for
*both sides* of the questions," both for and against. Thus in spite
of the talent for reasoning that Plato had to possess, his reasoning
is nevertheless "not any masterpiece," not as Socrates' was. But even
so, Plato is so much more than Socrates and all the "geometers"
under the sun that he quite simply "represents the privilege of the
intellect, of the power of mind."

To proceed. In his treatment of Shakespeare, Emerson demonstrates quite rightly that all originality is relative and every thinker
retrospective. He postulates the following: "Great men are more

distinguished by range and extent than by originality."[40] "It is easy
to see that what is best written and done by genius in the world is
not one man's work, but is wrought by the labor of thousands." And
he even introduces the Bible as support for this. On the other hand,
in his essay on Plato, which is in the same book and constitutes one
of the seven lectures comprising his major philosophical work, Emerson nevertheless maintains the diametrically opposite thesis. "Plato
is philosophy, and philosophy, Plato." "He has penetrated into
worlds which people of flesh and blood cannot reach." "In Plato
there is the germ of that Europe we know so well, in its long history
of arts and arms; here are all its stages mapped out beforehand in the
mind of Plato—*and by none before him.*"

Neither months nor years nor an altered philosophical outlook
lies between the first and the last statements quoted; in time three
weeks have passed and, in space, ninety-five octavo pages.

Having now very clearly shown how original Plato nevertheless
was—a man who had entered strange worlds and mapped out the
destiny of entire hemispheres in his mind, map work that none
before him had mapped out—Emerson again shifts ground, putting
his poor reader in a new predicament. The fact is that when one
gets right down to it, Emerson is not quite certain what Plato was
original about. His writings could just as well be someone else's
writings. To be sure, there were none before him, absolutely none,
but yet after all there could have been one or two before him. He
admits frankly: "When we are praising Plato, it seems we are praising quotations from Solon and Sophron and Philolaus." And he
adds: "Be it so. Every book is a quotation; and every house is a
quotation out of all forests and mines and stone quarries; and every
man is a quotation from all his ancestors."[41]

So the conclusion you finally arrive at is the following: Plato the
quotation sat in a quoted house and quoted the quotations Solon,
Sophron, and Philolaus in order to compose thereby a quotation
which *none before him* had any part or parcel in—yet remember
that according to Emerson's own words it is even "easy" to see that
the best writing is "wrought by the labor of thousands." But of
course Plato's writings reveal a writer who has "penetrated into

worlds which people of flesh and blood cannot reach." Well, if Plato himself did not produce his writings, how many people of flesh and blood would you guess remained on earth then when Plato's thousands of workers penetrated into other worlds? In Greece, at any rate, people of flesh and blood must have been pretty scarce in Plato's day. Only poor Socrates, it seems, was the kind of person—"an ignorant street debater"[42]—who still concerned himself with being flesh and blood.

Emerson cannot have read Plato without profit. He has found and appropriated his "two sides." These two sides then put him in a position to say the most two-sided things a philosopher has ever said in any country. This same man, who in one essay is ecstatic over this two-sidedness in Plato, declares just as ecstatically in another essay: "I love facts. An actually existent fly is more important than a possibly existent angel." And on both occasions that man has said an excellent thing.

Now what is Emerson's philosophy, finally and at last? Finally and at last Emerson's philosophy is exactly as it is now represented, and nothing more. It is a philosophy of over one hundred and fifty pages and can be purchased in England for a shilling—bound. It is a philosophy of "representative men." Shakespeare represents the poet, Montaigne the skeptic, Napoleon the man of the world, Goethe the writer, Swedenborg mysticism, and Plato philosophy. All these men were great men—therefore one can learn something from them. Emerson's study of Plato has led him to a certain point which, in spite of all his contradictions, stands firm for the reader, that is, a "fundamental unity: a God and an immortal soul." Now since it was Plato who in Emerson's eyes had invented both God and the soul, Plato is philosophy. Emerson has to have God; God is the most delectable word on his tongue. If he were a Scandinavian he would spell it *Guud.* In his philosophy, God and the soul are the sum total: there is a world; therefore there is a God. These pure truths are the major conclusions of Emerson's philosophical inquiries. This is the content of his essays.

In his efforts to prove the intimate connection between the soul and God, Emerson once again destroys his teaching on the relativity of originality. Whenever he comes close to divine territory, he develops Asiatic fits and it is goodbye to all of the theories he has propounded earlier. "The inviolate soul is in perpetual telegraphic communication with the source of events," he says. He expresses it even more clearly when he says, "The central fact is the superhuman intelligence pouring into us from its unknown fountain, to be received with religious awe, and defended from any mixture with our will." Then what is the use of all those "thousands of workers"? When the inviolate soul is pinched for information of one kind or another or an answer to some question, it does not even look the information up in Plato; "as a matter of fact," Emerson says, it comes to us firsthand from that unknown fountain, like a telegram. You feel wet just reading about this fountain that is supposed to pour into us. And if Emerson himself is afraid that the telegram might not materialize, he allows the Unitarian in him to add: "Verily we have no questions to ask which are unanswerable." Now, verily, this is a rather peculiar assertion from the mouth of a philosopher. Confronted with the most staggering enigmas, he stands still, fails to come up with anything, relaxes, and then bursts forth with the Psalmist. As for the immortality of the soul, Emerson then proves this with a line from Emerson: "If my bark sink, 'tis to another sea." In addition, he needlessly cites a couple of lines from Fox's views on eternity: And there is "an ocean of darkness and death; but withal an infinite ocean of light and love which flowed over that of darkness and death." Therefore the soul is immortal.[43]

With such ethical and philosophical trifles as these, Emerson has become a philosopher. These are his teachings: a soul in the body, a God on the horizon. What he asks of the philosophers is "wisdom," which he also interprets as "ethics." Plato's wisdom is boundless, Behmen's is "healthy and beautiful," Swedenborg's he finds "pleasant," Montaigne's "immoral," Shakespeare's "unbelievable"—in short, he asks what kind of wisdom it is and what it consists of. As if a serious philosophy were contingent on a specific morality! There are people who can as readily imagine a philosophy of vice as of virtue. Emerson's moral philosophy is just what you find in the homily collections of every Unitarian household (see the collec-

tions of sermons by Parker, Channing, and others). As far as that
goes, his philosophy is just what you find in all respectable people,
from good-natured messenger boys to honest whalingmen. Emerson
did not give moral philosophy a philosopher, but he did give it a
preacher. His intellectual makeup was preponderantly literary;
whether speaking or writing, he was genuinely talented. His countrymen take mottoes for their most ingenuous, goody-goody books
from his writings. He became the Aesop of the American mob of
moralists.

Even so, at times his literary talent has led him astray; it occurs
when he feels he ought to be profound. Now people are most assuredly used to many an incomprehensible sublimity in the writings
of philosophers, but it is especially interesting to see how a learned
Yankee behaves when he is being learned. A couple of Emerson's
oracular utterances that people have found profound sound like this:
"Knowledge is that knowing that we do not know." That is so true,
so very true! True enough, I do not understand a word of it, but
Emerson is absolutely right. You agree, do you not, that he would
have been wrong if he had said: Knowing is that knowledge that we
do not know? That is what you can do when you turn something
upside down. The other utterance is, if possible, even more remarkable: "Details are melancholy." Of course details are melancholy.
Every streetcar horse of average education knows that. Has anyone
ever heard that details were a chain of mountains or a window shade?
Well, there you are! I would just like to see anyone who could
say that details resemble melancholy less than any silk umbrella
anywhere in the whole world. Accordingly, details are melancholy. . . . .[44]

Ralph Waldo Emerson died in 1882.

There are of course additional American writers who would have
to be included in a literary history; the present work, however, does
not provide an occasion for meticulous selection. I have chosen to
give a slightly more detailed account of two American writers who
have become very well known here at home, in order to show just
how badly people can be deceived now and again when translating

by countries rather than by literatures. It is my purpose to show the kind of *intellectual climate* which a literature such as America's presupposes and fosters in a nation, that is, the seeds that are sown and the fruits that are harvested. Whitman and Emerson have been singled out as especially national representatives of their country's literature. This is not entirely advantageous to America, for the one was an inarticulate poet and the other a literary homilist. I do not for an instant doubt that American literature needs the influence of more advanced foreign literatures—literatures on which Congress patriotically imposes a duty. If American literature is to contribute to the nation's development, it must alter both its form and its content. But first *doubters* must arise in that big land, men and women who doubt that America possesses the greatest cultural riches in the world. The nation's smugness must be undermined, its patriotism severely jolted. Right up to this day the most sacred names in the country have been those of the Presidents! When one has some slight knowledge of the minds, the geniuses, that have inhabited the White House for several generations, this tells one a good deal about the nation that has canonized them. When Americans exact payment for admitting guidance in just those areas where they are behind, such action attests to the fact that there are absolutely no modern intellectual interests in the country.

# The Visual Arts

## PAINTING AND SCULPTURE

If we now turn to the visual arts in America, we get exactly the same impression—that is, they are an art form in need of guiding impulses from abroad. They too are fruits ripened in the nation's own materialistic climate, a climate infused with the spirit of the Boston clergy and sustained by the most massive patriotism imaginable. The Americans are a commercial nation devoted to buying and selling, not an artistic or art-loving nation. Their minds respond immediately to any kind of sale or money transaction that comes their way; the spirit of art, on the other hand, lies completely beyond their ken. They never allow themselves a day of quiet, and they never take time to listen. A true Yankee, one with the right national tastes, would much rather amuse himself with a patent report at the atheneum than attend a Wagnerian opera and, if it were not the thing to do, perhaps his wife and daughter would not attend either. Americans are not remotely *alert* or *responsive* to art. I am not asking them to discover art but to accept it, when it is offered to them, and to adapt it to their own national conditions, infusing it with new life. The Yankees are a young nation, but they are old enough to be moved, affected—at least attracted. Their scenery alone ought to have fostered an intelligent appreciation of beauty. Good heavens, they look at the sun and the sea—a sun peerless in any zone; they have white stars in the winter and red hurricane clouds on warm summer nights; a mysterious, rustling life of birdsongs, animal cries, and the stealthy tread of furry creatures stirs in their forests; a whole prairie world of color and fragrance and curious sounds swirls about their heads—but they do not notice it. Nothing can take their minds off figures; nothing of beauty can get them to forget the export trade and market prices for a single moment. In all those states, you can perhaps point to some exceptions in the course of a year, but not many—really very, very few. So it is not very strange that the level of American artistic endeavor is no higher than it is. These are the people, people with no appreciation of anything but making a living, to whom the country's art comes knocking; these are the people from whom it is to get encouragement. There is no use in asking for the slightest understanding, even if there were something to understand in American art; artists just have to put up with the most naive recognition and the most fatuous criticism. And at the exhibitions, finally, they are completely at the mercy of these people. Many a gentleman in America cannot tell a pastel from a chromo, much less one school from another; but if he knows the list of Presidents, if he knows the date of the famous battle of Atlanta, if he believes in God and has a million dollars, this alone is enough to get him a place on the jury at an art exhibition.

There are 88 art academies in America with 190 professors instructing three thousand students. Now this country, which has such ample means and whose art is so young, ought to employ *artists* as teachers at these academies, and they ought perhaps to do some slight screening of these three thousand students. But there is neither. Among American painters there are, as far as I know, three who have received medals in Europe or six who have won a name for themselves and deserve it. Undoubtedly it would be possible to scrape together half a score of talented artists from among their own ranks and then get the rest of the professors from other places, but that is really out of the question—things have to be kept American. Now the characteristic fact to be noted is that, as soon as an artist of real importance bobs up in America, he leaves his country just as soon as he can and goes to Europe. The restriction makers might take a hint from this, but they do not; they let the artists go. The upshot then is that the academies are left with men too old to travel and with young, aspiring dilettantes—who in turn are to teach young, aspiring dilettantes.

An American art exhibition is a bewildering sight. There is absolutely no selection made among the art works submitted; so you can find a masterpiece, a work of genius from a country with a rich art heritage, next to the most embarrassing display of talentlessness from the Dakota prairies. But then who makes the selection? In the great majority of cases the jury consists of the town mayor and a number of financiers—people who enjoy social respectability because they are wealthy and believe mightily in God but who are without background, without initiation in art—men who in the morning before taking their seats may get a few tips on aesthetics from a wife or daughter who has taken up painting herself. American painting is represented in the main by pictures of food: there are apples and grapes and pears and fish and all kinds of berries and plucked roosters and shanks of fresh beef all over the walls. Among these, there are large canvases in frames costing enormous sums; there can be frames ornamented with gold filigree. These pictures do not go to the galleries or art institutions; they are purchased by wealthy men for dining-room decorations. And since there is no secret about how these pictures are to be used, a whole industry suddenly opens up, a regular factory operation in roosters and beef shanks. These pictures are painted for the express purpose of being dining-room furnishings; they are decoratively executed with blazing colors and sharply defined figures so that they will look good on a wall. Even a beef shank is treated decoratively; often a lovely rosette or bow is tied around the stump of bone. A dead bird on a tray has its wings spread decoratively, each feather painted with wondrous colors. These dead wings fly across the tray so that they are a joy to behold. Now if these paintings are fairly well done, if they have a more or less familiar Yankee name in the corner, and if their frames are without spot or blemish, then of course very shortly they have their buyer—a wealthy man hangs these rarities up in his dining room.

Such an American jury has so little shame artistically that as a matter of course it also accepts the works of children *because* they are the works of children, giving them space anywhere, preferably in a spot that catches the eye. A card is hung on these childish scribblings indicating that the artist is twelve years old and an orphan. The card on a black-chalk drawing depicting two hens calls attention to the fact that the artist is fifteen, deaf, dumb, and lame. What has aesthetics to do with pity? As an artist I would not hesitate to kick the cripple's two hens off the wall. This drawing brazenly makes a fool of the viewer, and it besmirches the pictures in its vicinity. If anyone has once cast his eyes on this impossible picture, he can never forget it, never; it has left an impression just because of its embarrassing desperation; it has revolutionized itself into one's memory and there it stays. One cannot get rid of it. If ever in one's life one has seen a pair of such hens, they continue to this day to appear before one's eyes; they rise up just when one least expects them, they plop down on the paper when one is going to write, they perch on a lampshade, they cling to the calendar on the wall, woefully thrusting out legs so spindly that it tears one's heart to look at them.

There are also some good things among the bad at an American art exhibition, naturally, especially if the show encompasses the entire Union. The best in American art are landscapes; in that genre the country has its big and established names—men who have developed a regular routine in painting handsome oak trees. A genuine American landscape includes just exactly the following: a girl who milks a cow in a green meadow in front of a large forest against a blue mountain under a clear sky. This is a new expression of the moonlight found in literature. The American painters do these landscapes from memory: they never stumble over a straw; everything is smooth and flat. The cow has the same colors as a hummingbird, the forest is a forest of exceedingly decorative trees, and the mountains are so arranged that they neither weigh down the globe nor poke a hole in the heavens. Oh, one would like to take hold of those mountain tops and get them to bridle against the skies! And one would like to give that sky a cloud!

A pretty art of little daring, a flight into the blue, untouched by the world and what it contains, in spirit and content an art just like the literature. If a shepherd scene is depicted, everyone is wearing a great deal of clothing in that shepherd scene. The temperature can be 100 degrees and the grass withered from the heat, but the shepherd and shepherdess do not loosen a button. If an interior is depicted, "The Quiet Comforter" and George Washington are hanging on the wall, Sankey stands open on the piano, and the screw calendar under the mirror reads Sunday, August 23. And two people sit in this room on overstuffed chairs and are in love. Unbutton the buttons! Turn the calendar to Monday—a holiday Monday, a Monday of hooky—life's struggle and life's zest! I am not asking for madness and the great sin—that is a question of morals, an issue by itself. I am asking for life, for bodies alive in their clothes—that is a question of art. Let these two lovers show us that their pulses throb and their lungs breathe; let them show us that life struggles beneath their skins, that their bodies are enflamed with vitality!

Nothing but moonshine. Where American literature speaks with dashes, American art speaks with clothes. It has not come any further, and it will not come any further without guidance.

American sculpture is strongest in the field of animals: cats and dogs are their artists' first and final feat of daring; at most they do a Negro. An Indian in war dress, a crucified Christ, a bust of George Washington, appear repeatedly in American sculpture as examples of modern life. Now and again you run into a plaster-of-paris figure that catches your attention because there are a number of letters, a verse carved in the pedestal. The statue depicts a closely draped female figure of ineffable beauty, an American Venus with a waist as slender as a child's neck, and the verse calls attention to the fact that every woman can be that beautiful by buying and drinking a certain number of bottles of Ayer's Sarsaparilla. The plaster-of-paris figure is an advertisement for a patent medicine. Farther on you find a group piece—a housewife is washing the face of a half-grown boy, and a verse announces that everyone can be that clean by using a certain kind of soap for washing. The piece of art is an advertisement for Pears's soap factory in Brooklyn.

You do not approve of this profanation; perhaps it makes you angry that art can be made to serve publicity so directly—but in that very instant you remember what country you are in, and then you even give these plaster-of-paris figures your nod of approval. Why not? They are not without humor, and often they are quite clever creations. They have naturally very little artistic value: they are advertisements, store signs; but they are not moon lyrics, they render life, contain a situation, depict an action. On the other hand, what am I to do with an Indian for everyday use? An Indian does not even know that there is such a thing in life called soap. These art products used for advertising are the first steps towards an American national art; they correspond to journalism vis-à-vis literature and as such are the best, the most distinctive beginnings in art. American art strikes you as most remote from all noble ambition. To date, its very highest aspiration consists in rendering a dead and respectable President from the era of knee breeches or a more or less accurate copy of Venus de Milo. Of the President you know that his one real talent was his honesty and of Venus de Milo that the whole world has grown accustomed to kneeling at her feet. She stands in every window, knocks about on every shelf, rises up from every piano top, is present in every bankrupt estate, and is celebrated by every poet. In America she is the greatest figure a sculptor attempts to imitate; in Paris she is practically the Louvre. I am not taking into account her long neck, which could have been shorter, nor am I taking into account her drapery, which is a decoration, a drapery that conceals instead of covers; I take her as she stands there—a revelation. My feelings for her are a cry of aesthetic joy within me; she is a model of upright loveliness almost without flaw. But Venus de Milo is too remote from my soul. She could serve as a bookmark. I cannot think of one fish-market where I have met a woman whose face expressed so extraordinarily little as hers. When a person stands in some place, that person does so for one reason or another—Venus de Milo has absolutely no pressing need at all to stand there on her pedestal; she just does and is lovely, simply. Hers is a virginal, unyielding purity; if I touch her, I sully her. I do not love that woman; she takes away my illusions, robs me of all desire, fills me with a desolate sense of aesthetic pleasure that brings me no enrichment. An arm more, two more arms would simply give her figure the completeness it lacks—completeness in a human being who expresses so little. With a bit of affectation and feigned "artistic understanding" one can of course make her body come alive; in the next century impressionable people may even find arteries within her drapery.

Some years ago an American sculptor hit on the idea of doing his country a service; he was a Republican by political persuasion and a patriot by nature—there were those who felt that no other artist has ever been his equal. He carved a pedestal, a man standing upright, and a Negro kneeling; using cramp irons he put these three things together in a group. The man who stood upright was a slaveowner; he had a whip in his hand, and when an erect man holds a whip in his hand, he is without a doubt a slaveowner. The Negro was a slave; he is kneeling and praying, and when a Negro prays that is a marvel. And all America thought that this work was a marvel. The artist was a wag; like his countrymen he had a talent for thinking things up— he had carved the black Negro in white marble and the white slave-holder in black. *Uncle Tom's Cabin* all over again, *Uncle Tom's Cabin* exactly! Madam Stowe had not said more plainly in words what this group said in stone: what *black* barbarians the Southerners really were who could keep these *white* creatures on the cotton plantations to work for food, clothes, and wages. And the group presented an example of the courageous freedom and brotherly love shown by the Northern states when they set these people free. The artist was a patriot; from that time on he became a very important man, gaining a name for himself, recognition, a fortune, status. But his group did not disclose that the very same country that at the time freed a few thousand Negroes to this day keeps 1,119,000 of its own children as slaves in its own mines—no, the group did not disclose this.[*1] For it was not supposed to be a sermon against slavery

* The figure also includes the young children employed in the metal works—which are worse than the mines. The children are from six to fifteen. In just a single county (Luzerne), there are three thousand of these little ones employed in the coalmines. The average temperature in these mines is 95 degrees; the law stipulates how long the children are required to remain below ground at one time; they get virtually no schooling, and their wages do not correspond even proportionally to the wages that the Southern states pay their Negroes. (For statistics, see *North American Review*, 1884.) In the same country where child slavery is so unusually flourishing, people also defend

in general; that lay beyond its purpose. In the first place it was supposed to be a piece of political advertising for the Republican Party
to which the artist belonged;* in the second place it was supposed
to be a patriotic tribute to the entire country. And it was accepted as
such; it created a great stir and became the great monumental work
in the country's visual arts.

American sculpture is naturally also a very chaste art. Do not come
asking for human beings without a fig leaf! Even a naked child
playing with a shoe cannot, without a fig leaf, play with a shoe; in
fact if Dubois' *Eve* (*Eve nouveau-née*) were displayed in America,
she would not stand there long before getting a stomach warmer.
Throughout America's visual arts—as in literature—there is the most
prudish sensitivity about naked limbs. Artists have told me that they
have never painted from models, that they could not get hold of a
model either, because posing in the nude is so completely contrary
to the spirit of Boston, and that they certainly would not be allowed
to draw a model even if they had one. You can imagine what it is
like to proceed by conjecture, not just with the pores and changing
quality of the skin, but even with muscles and entire limbs. Is it any
wonder then that Venus de Milo emerges as the greatest, the most
daring temptation! Now take Ørsted Park in Copenhagen with its
naked statuary. A park like that, equipped with such a shortage of
fig leaves, would not be tolerated under any circumstances anywhere
in America—not even if a town got it free twice over. From Boston's
moral yammering, a harsh spirit of prudery goes drifting over
America, coloring and falsifying the general notions of both artist
and public. But while Americans are scrupulously afraid of an arm
without a sleeve or a calf without a stocking, they are nevertheless
unbelievably insensitive to the artistic, the spiritual, shamelessness
that pervades their art. In this I include both their detective stories
and their dining-room paintings—indeed, a good deal of their patri-

---

the immigration restrictions as a measure to protect American workers against
unemployment. What if the children were freed as the Negroes have been
freed? That measure would result in work for 700,000–800,000 grown men.

   * As is known, the other party, the Democrats, opposed the war.

otic sculpture as well. No one balks at serving up impossible hens to visitors at an exhibition, hung there simply because a cripple has conceived these hens, and they find it perfectly natural that viewers gather around this drawing. You see the most comical pictures for sale at art dealers', such as wild moose in the mountains, each with a silk ribbon around its antlers, or a single, brilliant star seen through the window of a cottage where everything else is in daylight. Three years ago in St. Louis, the capital of Missouri and one of the Union's largest transportation centers, a group of chromo pictures was exhibited that contained gilded water, sky-blue sheep, and people with eyes of rosy pink. When art becomes original in this manner, the viewer of course falls silent; he is struck dumb. Just as long as he does not smile—it is all meant to be taken seriously. He is standing on American soil observing an American art event, and he has to appreciate the revelations of art, whatever they may be, with the same reverence that he appreciates the music of patriotic penny whistles that go piping through the streets.

Much of the prudery in American art can be explained by the fact that the great majority of those engaged in painting are *women*. This is significant; it is a key explanation for the artistic tastes of the entire nation. American women are the leaders of art in their country just as the German women now lead *their* literature—and desolate it with the dexterity of their pens. Either they are rich men's daughters who have learned their art at one of the eighty-eight American academies, or they are married women who on their own initiative, out of boredom and because it is the proper thing to do, have turned to dabbling at home. Making paintings is quite simply feminine handiwork; you do not have to visit very many homes over there before this becomes apparent. It almost seems as if American women feel that they owe it to themselves to bring a couple of hens into the world. The influence of women, which in turn is shaped by the temper of Boston, is so prevalent that it affects all of the country's art. And not only the painters and sculptors but also the writers and actors come under its sway. In America the women call the tune.

Let me remind you again that it is useless to try to excuse American art by saying that no one yet expects it to have progressed further than it has. That is taken as an insult, and you are asked to come and try to make something of it. For there are no doubters in America, no clouds in the American skies. There is no vital awareness of the fact that the country's art needs both impulses and direction from abroad; they charge two and a quarter million a year to accept instruction. People answered me over there by saying that there was presumably a duty on art in Europe too. This objection was made without irony, in absolute good faith; the Yankees could not go any further in their thinking. Of course there is not a country in Europe that is not better situated than America to do without foreign art imports, and—still more important—there is not one country in Europe that economically is so well situated as America to do without the duty. The amount of idle money in the U.S. Treasury is so enormous that, if it were all released at one time, it would completely disrupt the country's business economy. There is so much money that even the Americans are staggered by it; they do not know how on earth to invest it. As is known, this money has become a bone of contention in America's domestic politics.

Someone might wish to remark that nevertheless there has recently been a certain national consensus for a significant reduction in the duty on art products. It is of interest to examine the strength of this consensus. In reality it is no stronger than in 1846. My impression of this last tariff bill is exactly the same as it is of all its predecessors. For this is not the first time in that country of America that such a bill has appeared. A bill passed by one session of the Congress can be completely or partially nullified by the next, depending upon the political stripe of the President or Senate in power. In 1842 the American import duty on art objects was 30 percent; in 1846 it was reduced to 20 percent; in 1857 the duty was removed completely. This lasted for four years. In 1861 the duty was again set at 10 percent. But the Congress of 1883 took a tremendously patriotic step; it wanted to "protect" the country's own art and show the world its independence; so it saddled foreign art with no less than a 35 percent import duty—a duty worse than ever before. And there it remains. Tariff bills come and go with practically every presidential election in America; it is best not to regard them unequivocally as favorable signs of progress: they are transitory, products of the shifting political situation. Far from being an expression of Americans' awakening desire for artistic impulses from abroad, this latest bill to reduce the duty on art is simply a necessary consequence of the general reduction of tariffs in the United States. It was a question of reducing the cash reserves in the national treasury at a single stroke, and when fortune rained on French wines and Chinese porcelain, it also dripped on art. Bills like that come and go in the republic; they are the election maneuverings of this or that political party and arise not for the sake of art but for French wine and Chinese porcelain.

No, the truth is that Americans are unaware of the larger artistic context; it is a country in which art means dining-room decorations. If we are reminded that there is after all a market for European art in America, the case is the same as with the Americans' weakness for European titles and decorations; these democratic people are not, you see, indifferent to such things. In Washington, Boston, and New York this sickly craving for social status is just as prevalent an illness as toothaches and nerves. If you ask to see the autograph album of a fashionable lady in Washington, D.C., you will discover how many people of rank she counts among her acquaintances; there are names embellished with the most curious titles. On my last trip home from America, I traveled with a woman from New York whose sole errand in Europe was to dig up some minor title for a great-great grandfather in order by this means to gain entrance to the aristocracy of New York. Without a new visiting card it was useless for her to apply; she was not rich enough. This is also the case with America as a market for European art. An American, then, is deemed rich only when he has a Swiss mountain or an Italian shepherd in his salon; this gives the house status, a title. But it is a title that does not ennoble. These art-buying Americans have had enough money to take a trip to Europe with their families in order to complete, at hotels in Paris and on steamboats on the Rhine, an education which has in reality never begun.[2] They then bring back a couple of pictures from this trip; in America it is fashionable to have such mementos from one's travels. The following year the same family makes a trip in its own country and brings back a lump of ore from California and an

Indian pipe from Wyoming—again mementos that are also fashionable to own. The one is just as good as the other.

Americans have money for art; consequently they buy art. But they have no background in art, no craving for art. There have been official plans published in America regarding means of keeping European art at arm's length; leading periodicals have discussed the issue.*³ And when this can happen in a country with such art as America's, it is because the level of cultural development is lower in that country than the nation itself realizes.

* To mention just one example, I refer to the *International Review,* 1879.

# Dramatic Art

## I. Plays and Players

The art in which America has shown the greatest achievement is undoubtedly dramatic art. Over there you find good actors in farce, performers of even outstanding talent in that crude comedy of the buffoon. The Americans possess—except in their literature and a portion of their visual arts—a well-developed realistic sense; their stages seethe with life. They drive locomotives, sail steamboats, ride fiery steeds, shoot off cannons, and fire guns—good heavens, the shooting! Often the reek of gunsmoke is almost unbearable for the poor spectators. All the tumult of life that the American newspapers are full of reappears on the American stage. But of course there is too little artistry in this savage din; the raw power used to generate the effect is too great. Then the effect is driven away on a locomotive and shot down with cannons.

Throughout America there are but two and at the most three theaters that have a permanent company of actors; otherwise the theaters are hired by traveling companies for one or more nights, as a rule for a week at a time. These companies travel all year round with the same play. When in the course of the year they have played every American stage, they repeat the tour the following year, beginning at the Atlantic Ocean and ending out on the Pacific coast. There is not much opportunity in these wandering troupes for making the most of one's talents; one does as the poets do who learn their craft once and for all. It is therefore all the more remarkable that, under such circumstances, talented and influential actors have appeared in America. Besides a couple of opera singers, who of course have been educated in Europe and whose training therefore has been constantly subject to foreign influence, there are three distinguished tragedians who have received their education almost exclusively on American soil—that is, Kean, Booth, and Murphey.

The latter two have achieved a high degree of success in imitating European Shakespearean performers, and this in itself is a great and happy achievement in a country like America, where there are such stout defenses against all foreign artistic influence. Booth, moreover, has had to overcome the antipathy of an entire nation during his artistic career, for it was his brother who murdered Abraham Lincoln —and this of course somewhat impeded his acceptance as an artist. Edwin Booth also performs less often now. He has amassed a large fortune through his acting; also, he has become old. Otherwise he lives such an irregular life that for this reason as well he is getting to be more and more impossible. He has a robust nature and in his art he is something of a butcher. In his personal life he loves the coarser pleasures: he is a drunkard. You can see him intoxicated in the grandest roles, but he acts superbly as long as he does not lapse into carelessness.

Were one to make a comment about Murphey's peculiarities as an artist, it would have to be that in spite of his really intelligent readings of several Shakespearean roles, he is on stage too much, he takes up too much room, and he seems to have too much steam—a peculiarity that is an innate gift of God, since he is an Irish-American. Actor Murphey acts entirely too much: he is Richard the Third in the sweat of his brow; he is forever and a day playing Henry the Fifth. But just for this reason he is perhaps even better understood by his public. His art is somewhat American, but then he is also performing for Americans.

It can be said of Kean, on the other hand, that this refined, appealing, long-haired gentleman has created a completely new and original Hamlet. Kean's is a profoundly original nature, and there is perhaps not a single feature of his Hamlet which is borrowed from others; for this reason it is also an intense pleasure to see him in that role. One looks in amazement at a friend whom one does not recognize, and in those scenes where his mind is in a turmoil one shudders with delight at his mysterious art. For time and again the Hamlet role has cost him his sanity; he has been in a mental institution three or four times; every time he comes out again he goes on the boards and plays Hamlet—as long as it lasts. He is demented with the fixed idea that he is nothing—at most a speck of dust, a pinpoint. Other than he there are not very many Americans who have this fixed idea! There is a fearsome reality in Kean's acting; his eyes resemble two slits, and one sees very plainly how the madness lurks beneath his brow. He has performed in England, but they did not understand him in England; there is not enough beef in his art. He has to turn to his own countrymen, among whom only the best understand him. Of all the men I have met in America, I have never found such an intensely artistic nature as Kean's. That man not only portrays tragedy, tragic men and tragic life, even his portrayal of tragedy becomes tragic because one sees and hears the hectic undercurrent of madness in his art. One views, so to speak, two tragedies in Kean's interpretation of Hamlet—Hamlet's tragedy and the portrayer's. And when Kean stands on stage and is possessed by his art, his own tragedy is no less interesting than Shakespeare's at times somewhat ponderous tragic clamor. In Kean, art is a natural force: he was born with it—and he will doubtless sometime die of it.[1]

Unfortunately America does not have additional actors of Kean's stature. But America has many actors. On the whole, the Irish are the most competent. These gifted, quick-witted, apt, and thievish Irish immigrants have become the best actors in the country. In farce an Irishman is indispensable; there is a regular profession for Irishmen in farce—the professional Irishman. In the dramatizations of detective stories he is the policeman who makes all the discoveries; in the patriotic war plays he is the spy who penetrates the secrets of the Southern states; in serious drama he comes forward at the eleventh hour like a rescuing angel; in the romantic pieces he is rich and plays providence for the two lovers—the success of a play turns absolutely on a good Irishman. Being an Irishman is a role. And the actor in that role must have such a brogue that he barely can be understood;

moreover he must always have red hair, be clean-shaven, and able to do the jig. In an American play the Irishman provides the fun and change of pace after the insipid action of the love story has gone on for a full fifteen minutes. So it is gratifying to play an Irishman; he is almost always jubilantly received by the entire house when he dashes in.

Except for the few exceptions, you encounter very primitive dramatic art in American theaters. Too much of it resembles country-fair entertainment. The level of performance is about the same throughout the nation. I have seen things at the Grand in New York that have later played at second-run theaters in Chicago, and I have seen things on second-rate stages in Chicago that have played the Grand in Boston. Even on Chicago's largest stage you very frequently find entertainment that no one would dare to present at the smallest provincial theater here at home. The problem is not so much with the actors as with the plays. The American stage has many capable actors who in their entire lives are never asked to do anything more challenging than play an Irishman or a Negro. A truly American play simply does not hang together from start to finish; it consists of innumerable scenes that constitute small individual plays, bearing no necessary relationship to those coming before or after. Achieving a total effect is not important—except perhaps when a locomotive is allowed to go whizzing across the stage after the final line; what is important is to stage the various situations in such a way that each has an impact on the spectators, making them clap, laugh, or cry. This depends less on the play's coherence than on entertaining dialogue and action favorable to the appearance of an Irishman. A play with a beginning and an end, a dramatic work, is very rarely seen in an American theater; as a result they make plays out of the most inconceivable things. To keep from mentioning *Uncle Tom's Cabin, Oliver Twist,* and *The Battle for Atlanta,* the Americans even make a play of the Chicago anarchists; they could make a play of the city directory, of two hens, of the Suez Canal; they could dramatize the multiplication tables. There is no end to the things that Yankees could make plays of.

The American play is farce—farce with all the trappings. Next

to a good Irishman, it is a question of having the most insane sound
effects for bombardments and scenes of bloodshed; after these,
finally, comes the decor. The sets are such an important part of an
American play that they are mentioned in boldface type on the
playbill; they are called "realistic scenery." New costumes for the
cast get special notice, and the value of the prima donna's jewelry
is given. The playbills always say that never before have such
sumptuously magnificent sets been seen in town; for this reason it is
anticipated that everyone will come to see this gem of a play. Now
since the sets mean so much to an American play, and furthermore
since everyone knows that the Americans' most highly developed
faculty is their technical skill, you would expect them to produce
some totally undreamed of marvels in the line of sets. But this is not
necessarily the case. Either they lack the artistry to harmonize the
staging with the play itself, or they do not even have enough taste to
coordinate the various parts of the sets. At the best theater in New
York, I attended a play so lavishly staged that the sets were an
absolute triumph. There were mountains such as I have never seen
surpassed in Norway, a pasteboard forest, pasteboard animals, pasteboard birds, and a pasteboard elephant as large as—a watch key.
Everything was made of the stiffest, the most lifeless pasteboard
imaginable. In the midst of this pasteboard world, however, an
evening sun was shining that from a technical standpoint was a real
work of art. It captured the light in America's sun and tricked the
spectator into forgetting where he was; with truly deceptive naturalness it captured the changing luster of the sun as it gradually sank.
It poured light forth in every direction, like froth billowing out over
the landscape. The sun slips lower and lower; the light dims; the
hypnotic, brassy sheen gives way and is tarnished a dull gold. The
sun slips lower and lower; the light grows cold and red; bloody and
quenched, it seeps over the mountain tops. It turns a greenish hue;
it takes on the appearance of woven velvet; it grows furry. And the
sun slips lower and lower . . . . . Such a sun was allowed to cast
its light on a pasteboard landscape, on mountains and rivers that
shivered and shook if a skirt but fluttered in the wings. It was an

artistic wasteland in sunlight! The landscape was stone-dead; the only thing alive in it, aside from the sun, was a man. This man was going to cross one of the mountains in the background, for his sweetheart lived on the other side of that mountain. So he started walking. Now when a man is going to cross a mountain and this man is in full possession of his senses, he proceeds as much as possible in the same direction. But not this man. In order to prove to the audience that he was walking, he strode this way and that in the pasteboard forest, past pasteboard birds that did not move an inch, past a rock whose very foundation shook at his step; he crossed a pasteboard creek without getting his feet wet; he rushed past the watch key, turned back, all the time walking like fury, like a man possessed, this way and that, that way and this—until he finally disappeared into the wings. Then at last the sun sank to the accompaniment of soft music, and night fell. A scene passed, an eight-minute scene. In the immediately following episode the man had already returned, and in a monologue half a mile long he then related to the audience and himself how he now had the long trek from the other side of the mountains behind him—an account everyone in the theater knew for dead certain was *not* true!

The Americans are totally unacquainted with a *sliding* scene which makes it possible for a man who is going to cross a mountain to proceed in one direction for a full thirty minutes without bumping his nose against a backdrop or running into the wings.[2]

Often so-called "French" plays run at American theaters; it goes without saying that the plays have never seen France. From the newspapers the Americans have simply caught wind of the fact that French dramatic art is not so hopelessly far behind Dakota's—so the Americans produce French plays. In these plays, which are always extravagantly staged, you can see the same scenery used for a galley-slave colony in Toulon and a middle-class home in Marseille, both in the same play; and in somewhat less French, that is, somewhat more American, productions you can see the same background used for a Turkish harem and an American saloon. Americans do not operate on the assumption that a set need absolutely suit the play at hand. If they have come up with something attractive, they use it without a second thought, regardless of whether the play is a prairie adventure or a drama of city life.

When you get somewhat better acquainted with it, you do not have the greatest confidence in the Americans' sense of decor—it shows very little refinement and no schooling. If Americans could picture the art of decor created by Ludvig of Bavaria, if they could but begin to imagine anything so delightfully seductive as the sliding fairy landscapes in *Urvasi,* they would perhaps speak in smaller letters about their own sumptuously magnificent pasteboard forests. But the Yankees know nothing about that kind of art, and they do not want to know; they are not willing to be instructed in this field either. Their smugness is consistent throughout.

## II. Hostility to Foreigners

Now and again our newspapers report that on one date Ibsen's *Ghosts* was produced in New York City and that on another Sardou was performed in one of the western cities. These are half-truths. I speak somewhat from personal experience, somewhat from inside knowledge. *Ghosts* has *never* been staged in New York and Sardou has *never* been performed in a single American city.* With *Ghosts,* only those scenes that caused no objections were performed in New York; all the ghosts were "sifted" out of the drama, and it was staged in a form that was totally unrecognizable. To show how brutally this play was distorted from an artistic standpoint, I need only mention that some lines of verse were appended to the final scene, which had already been mutilated—lines with which Mrs. Alving was then supposed to entertain the audience before the curtain fell. The statement that *Ghosts* has been staged in New York can thus only very generously be described as a half-truth. As for Sardou, I have seen his name on American playbills several times, but if you conclude from this that Sardou also has really been performed, you are very

* Except when Sarah Bernhardt has had Sardou plays in her tour repertoire.

greatly mistaken. The same thing happens to him as to Ibsen: his dramas are sifted. They are taken apart and broken up, then made into countless scenes and supplied with a role for an Irishman involving either some verse or a jig. Genuine Sardou plays have not been produced on a single American stage—not in the English language and by Americans.

If one could substantiate the story that even Ibsen, even Sardou and Dumas have been and are being performed in America, one could also prove immediately that the American theater is a modern theater animated by the spirit of the age. An import duty on foreign dramatic works would then simply be an economic question involving the nation's treasury. But this import duty is not first and foremost an economic question involving the nation's treasury. It is first and foremost an expression of the nation's sense of self-sufficiency. In reality the American people are also very hostile to modern dramatic art. How then do people over there react when, for example, Sarah Bernhardt comes? They make a big fuss about the ticket prices, about her not having bothered to learn English, about her being, when you get right down to it, a half-mad female from whom sensible people can learn nothing. They go even further. The press tells all the mothers in town to beware of the "crazy one." She has a snake along, the press reports; at night she sleeps with this snake on her breast, and she is capable at any moment of letting this snake slip loose. The press goes even further. For sacred patriotic reasons it advises the public not to pay these high prices to a foreigner but instead to save their money until a later date when a truly national pasteboard forest will be playing. Is that all then? Absolutely not! The press warns all respectable people against going to see Sarah Bernhardt; for in regard to Sarah Bernhardt, the press reports, Sarah Bernhardt has had an illegitimate child. Unfortunately she is not socially acceptable; she is practically a common prostitute. You can check the accuracy of my account in, among other places, Minneapolis—the city the size of Copenhagen—where this warning against Sarah Bernhardt's art appeared in the city's largest newspaper in June 1886.

It is not true that great and mature dramatic art has free access to

America any more than that modern art is welcome there. At any rate it must be an art that reflects the common Boston morality; otherwise it is sifted, mutilated, and Americanized. Recently a strong movement has got underway in Yankeeland whose purpose, no less, is to prevent foreign actors from performing in America by means of enormous tariffs. In December a delegation of American actors appeared before the Immigration Committee and applied for protection against the influx of modern dramatic art. The movement is certain to leave its mark on the new tariff law in the United States. A couple of large newspapers in the East, the *New York Herald* and the *Evening Post,* have expressed their opposition to this most recent outburst of patriotic aesthetics, but not for artistic reasons, merely political. Both of these papers, you see, are proponents of free trade, and as such they have to combat every sign of protectionism, however it manifests itself. The *New York Herald* even writes: "We do not look upon protective tariffs as a blessing for us, but if we have got to have them, then let us go all the way." A movement led by America's best-known actors, Booth, Jefferson, Barrett, and a mediocrity by the name of Boucicault, is certain to have its effect. I have searched for Kean's name among these patriotic actors, but it is not there—again evidence of the nobility of Kean's artistic spirit. Boucicault, on the other hand—a man whom every worthwhile theater would simply be better off without—talks and writes as though he were the greatest drama expert in the country. "I foresee the day," he states, "when people in London will organize acting troupes that will go on tour in the United States. And as our dear countrymen always prefer what is foreign (!), there will be nothing left for American actors to do but take to the prairies and if possible see to earning the bare essentials of life." And Boucicault goes on to say from New York: "I don't see why, if the trades and industries of this country are to be protected in regard to imported labor, our profession should be exempt. I believe the movement we now have started is a marvelous one, and I hope we can carry it through. The pushing to the forefront of English or other European actors and actresses is simply to give the American public a slap in the face. The American actors and actresses are without exception the best in the world, but I know that hundreds of them have been prevented from making a living because of foreigners. If I were to organize a theatrical company and wished it to be perfect in all respects, I should select Americans for every single phase."

The journal *America* appends the following comment to these words of wisdom: "Our actors are absolutely right in their efforts. Dion Boucicault has expressed the opinion and sentiments of the true American, and his words have the greatest weight as coming from a man who is in a position to know whereof he speaks."[3]

Thus what little dramatic art Europe hitherto has been granted the honor of teaching America is well on its way to being destroyed. And whooping with joy, the actors of the country go charging off into the most marvelous kind of retrogression. But a single artist remains behind, the greatest of them all, Kean.

Shakespeare is the only dramatist whose works, in contrast to Ibsen's and Sardou's, the Americans attempt to produce in toto. The reason the Yankees make this exception for Shakespeare can be explained in a few words. Shakespeare is the universal genius, the grand old master. There is a brutal simplification in Shakespeare's depiction of human emotions that makes them quite different from our own: his portrayals of love, wrath, desperation, and merriment fail to come off from sheer violence. We recognize these uncompromising emotions without shading or nuance as belonging to a bygone age when men still frothed at the mouth—consequently Shakespeare is not a modern psychologist. My own modest opinion is therefore not that Shakespeare is too old; my modest opinion is that he is old. There is too little complexity in his depiction of the emotions which, without pause for accident or contradiction, head straight for the abyss of extremes. Hamlet's psychology is an oasis, but there are desolate spots in that oasis. Shakespeare's plays are again just as simple, just as uncomplicated as the emotions he portrays; they are very often naive in comparison with the work of modern dramatists. The most marvelous things happen in *Othello*, for example, simply because a handkerchief falls on the floor. Shakespeare is not a modern dramatist, but a dramatist he will remain until the end of time.

As a result Shakespeare is performed on American stages, first, because he is the grand old master who is performed everywhere under the sun; second, because he is an antique, since his writings originated prior to 1700; and, third, because in America he is considered half-American, that is, a national possession. When you know that the Yankees have virtually gone so far as to make even Napoleon III into an American, there is nothing particularly surprising about Shakespeare's having also suffered the same fate. He has been deemed worthy; people feel he really deserves it. His picture therefore is also hung above the stage. Why shouldn't his picture be hung above the stage? Shakespeare was a man whom no nation need feel ashamed of. Certain rights are nevertheless reserved. If people are to have a foreigner hanging above their stage or, at any rate, someone whose actual American birth could be contested, then they also want a couple of others up there who not a living soul will doubt were Americans; and so they hang up a couple of others. Now since America does not have any dramatists, you would think that the greatest actors in the country are the obvious choice for this spot beside Shakespeare. But they are not the ones you see, not Kean or Booth or Mary Anderson. *George Washington* and *Abraham Lincoln* are the ones that hang there with Shakespeare between them. When people see this, they naturally have the feeling that Shakespeare has come into very good company artistically. This is just patriotism anew. An American stage is not supposed to devote itself primarily to the production of those works that stir our age and world; it is supposed to peddle *American* wares primarily. The stage is supposed to be patriotic; it is even supposed to be Republican or Democratic in its political orientation. At Fourth of July performances you sometimes have, virtually at the risk of your life, an opportunity to see just how patriotic the American stage actually is.

Time and again when I have been at an American theater, just sitting there bored, reading the advertisements in the program, I have been rudely jolted out of my indifference by a sudden swell of applause that has rocked the entire theater with cheers and clapping. What is happening? I glance up at the stage—no, nothing unusual; a man is standing there delivering a monologue half a mile long. So in even greater amazement I ask my neighbor what is going on. "It's," my neighbor says, clapping so hard that he can barely speak, "it's, it's George Washington," he says. It now turns out that the man up there on the stage has actually mentioned George Washington's name in the course of his monologue. That was enough—more than enough. That entire mass of people has been electrified, and the din is worse than in a boiler works. People are whooping and shouting; they bang their umbrellas and canes on the floor, shoot paper wads at those not joining in, throw handkerchiefs, and whistle—all because of George Washington's name. Now you would certainly think that people could hear that name without taking leave of their senses for five minutes, but you do so only if you are unacquainted with American patriotism. For you see Americans are so fiercely patriotic that not even their dramatic art can escape damage from this embarrassing influence. This is art—this monologue that mentions George Washington by name! And it is simply one's civic and human duty to clap when one hears that name.

It is precisely this that the American theater lacks—a serious *dedication to art*. There is useable theater talent and there are Shakespearean dramas, but there is no serious dedication. You feel the absence of this artistic seriousness the moment you enter an American theater. You do not find yourself in an educational institution or a temple of culture but at an extravagently mounted side-show, confronted with tricky staging and clever Irish witticisms. There are constant disturbances. Cigar butts and nutshells come raining down on your head from the gallery, and waiters, carrying trays of water and bags of candy, go racing around shouting. People are buying and selling things; they jingle their money, whisper, and talk out loud as they tell each other about market prices and the wheat harvest. Then a man comes along and passes out next week's program, which is an exact replica of an American bank check and reflects the same level of taste as everything else.[4] The whole thing is business, cheap entertainment, and bad taste.

Nor does this public feel that it shares any responsibility, artistically, for the accidents and far too conspicuous errors that occur on stage. These people make no demands on art because they have no background in it; they want to be entertained and hear about patriotism. There is thus extremely little outside influence that can spur these actors into doing their best. They cannot expect many to understand their work and even fewer to appraise it critically. As a result, performances far too often display the obvious signs of these circumstances. The actors feed each other cues in loud voices, and the audience generally laughs at this. Theodora may be lying stone-dead on her couch and yet she opens and closes her eyes—and the audience generally laughs at this. No one boos the actors if they intentionally, in order to rouse a laugh, tear dramatic illusion to shreds after it has been painstakingly built up. On the contrary. On the American stage no one hesitates to rob the spectator of his illusions. I saw a gentleman go bareheaded on the street in *Oliver Twist*. The scene was a street in London, but the man who played Oliver's benefactor obviously wanted his public to know that he was a man with good manners. For this reason he chose to leave his hat at home when he went out on the streets of London to perform his benefactions. I saw the following in a patriotic play: the scene is a military camp; a young soldier has arrived in camp; he is an Irishman, that is, a spy. He makes some important discoveries and is determined to get a dispatch off to his friends in the other camp. But there is no opportunity, naturally. So he takes a bow that is lying on the floor—Why, by the way, is a bow lying on the floor? This is not an Indian war; it is a modern war with rifles. Never mind, he takes this bow, sticks the dispatch on the arrow, puts this in place, and shoots. The arrow fell to the floor. The arrow did fall to the floor. We all sat there and saw it; the arrow dropped right to the floor. Well, do you suppose people thought that was any reason for the arrow not to reach the other camp? Not in your life! The Irishman had a man standing there who described the course of the arrow. It bored its way farther and farther into the air, piercing the ether like a sliver, flashing as it sped along—until it finally fell right at the feet of his friends in the other camp. Those Yankees clapped from every seat in the house— the North was saved! As for the arrow, it lay on the floor. That was no accident with the arrow, for I took it upon myself to check its performance. The play continued night after night, but the arrow did not get any better. As soon as it was shot off, it fell to the floor. But since it sped four and a half miles through the air anyway, there was no reason to make a fuss. No one did either.

Another thing that destroys all sense of theatrical illusion is the custom of changing the scenery right in front of the audience with the lights turned up. These changes are made on an open stage even when there is absolutely no call for it; in other words, they are *always* done this way. When you know how an American play is put together, that is, with countless unrelated scenes of the most varied content, you can imagine how often these exposed scenery changes take place. Invariably as you sit there you lose all sense of illusion. You sit there looking at a scene representing a street in San Francisco. And just as things are going well, two men walk behind the set and each drags off his half of the street in San Francisco with everyone watching. Not a lamp is dimmed. The next scene takes place along the Mississippi. When the scene is shifted, the river is divided, and each half is dragged off so that the waters are like a wall on the right hand and on the left—as it is written. Not a lamp is dimmed. There the electric lights are, frantically flooding the destruction with their brilliance.

Thus American dramatic art could also do with a measure of artistic dedication, a measure of intelligence—a breath of pure art.

# The Cultural Harvest

## I. Concepts of Freedom

For a long time it has been common journalistic practice here at home to use American freedom as an illustration of what freedom is and ought to be. The gentlemen of the press know so little what they do! The Liberals boast on principle; the Conservatives protest out of habit—an incessant clip-snip which only in the rarest instances builds on personal experience.

Just drawing together the casual impressions mentioned thus far, we find that American *intellectual* freedom has manifested itself as follows: it punishes a newspaper for admitting that Congress has committed a piece of parliamentary stupidity; it forces a common-school pupil to beg Jesus for forgiveness because he has thrown paper wads in an arithmetic period; it rebukes an author by boycotting him because he has exposed some of the humbug connected with American female virtue; it silences another author because his books show signs of European influence; it puts a 35 percent import duty on modern culture; it mutilates Zola's books and refuses to tolerate them in bookstores;* it prohibits a painter from depicting shepherds that are not all buttoned up; it attacks Sarah Bernhardt's honor because this artist, as a human being, has loosened a button—just these few instances chosen at random give a fairly good idea of the nature of American intellectual freedom.

* In October it finally became unlawful to import *La Terre* "by reason of its immorality."

If we now turn to *social* freedom, a couple of those features already noted will also serve to illustrate it: for example, it is a civic duty to clap for George Washington's name; people can with impunity fire nutshells and cigar butts at a man in a public place because he does not go into raptures at the sound of that name; an immigrant very frequently has to deny his foreign origin if a Yankee is to hire him; at the same time that a few thousand African half-apes were freed, more than a million white children were held in legally protected slavery; finally, a woman without money or title does not have access to certain American homes. It is a trifle naive to set such freedom up as a model for freedom in general: it is conditional freedom.

In the first place, freedom in America is very disproportionate and inharmonious—like everything else in the country. You notice immediately that it is not the product of a gradual, progressive development but in many areas simply the result of precipitous congressional decision. It has no form; it is without balance or continuity. Life is so free in America that you can shoot a man down on the open street for having cursed in a shop when a lady was present, but life is not so free in America that you can spit on the floor where you please or go with a lighted cigar—that is not true! American freedom is just as ridiculously exacting and restrictive about little things as, indeed, according to the Constitution it is generous and liberal about big things. When, for example, an immigrant goes ashore in New York, his knife is taken from him immediately—a knife that he wears in a sheath and uses for shredding his pipe tobacco; but he is allowed to carry a revolver in both hip pockets if he wants to, for the revolver is the national murder weapon.

Furthermore, freedom in America is not always voluntary but often compulsory, a freedom dictated by law. Congress sits and makes laws governing how free the individual is obliged to be instead of simply determining how free he may *not* be. You come up against a number of instances of freedom that are dictated by law in America. Washington's birthday is thus a prescribed public holiday that each year disrupts school instruction far more than any religious holiday; but on that day you are obliged to be free. In 1868 a writer bobbed up in the republic who wrote that he believed in monarchy; the man's name was Fred Nicolls and his book was called *Thoughts*.[1] Things did not go well for that man; he had not felt obliged to be free. His treatment by the newspapers and at public gatherings was such that he felt he could take a trip down to Mexico with a clear conscience—and he has never returned. Behold, even a man's thoughts are required to contain a certain measure of American freedom; otherwise he finds that he has an errand in Mexico. In addition to this freedom dictated by law, there is the kind of compulsory freedom that these patriotic people have prescribed for themselves. You can be certain that a merchant who does not close his shop on the Fourth of July has to pay for it in one way or another; a man seated in a theater who fails to lose his head over George Washington's name also has to pay for it. A foreigner does not feel unconditionally free right there in America—his tastes and opinions are dictated to him, and he simply has to acquiesce or take the consequences. He is faced with the despotism of freedom—a despotism that is all the more intolerable because it is exercised by a self-righteous, unintelligent people. In America no distinction is made between freedom and democracy; in order to maintain a compact democracy, freedom is willingly sacrificed. That noble, ardent craving of the individual for freedom is wounded in many different ways. By undermining all individual yearning for freedom in its citizens, America has finally managed to create that horde of fanatic freedom automatons which make up American democracy.

Last of all, there are great, open holes in American freedom which, even in formal terms, is greatly inferior to conditions in several other countries. This is particularly true of those areas in which religious stupidity and patriotic fanaticism operate hand in hand. I want to tell you about an important and characteristic instance of American intellectual and social freedom that is both accurate as an example and illustrative as a picture—an instance that will at the same time begin to explain the spirit pervading American legal justice.

The following paragraph occurs in the proposals for restricting immigration: "Socialists, anarchists, and nihilists are forbidden to land . . . because these people stir up the American working population and make it dissatisfied with wages. America is not the place

for socialistic propaganda." The truth is, America is not the place
for cultural and sociopolitical development; it stands where it stood
on that blessed day of national independence. Mention the word
*anarchism* in America, and a man with an ordinary, average American education crosses himself immediately. He conceives of anarchism as dynamite simply, nothing but dynamite. That anarchism is
a scientific theory, a doctrine, which even halfway sensible people
profess is beyond him; he cannot stand to hear a word about it.
Anarchism is dynamite; anarchists are to be hanged! Here is a gap-
ing hole in American freedom, a hole held open by just that thick-
skulled democracy whose control of freedom in America is absolute.
During the great anarchist trial in 1886, the hole quite simply wid-
ened into an abyss. At the time, people of every social class—from
those who by some stroke of luck had made millions on wheat
swindles to those who could not read or write their own name—that
is, all Americans went around and privately condemned these seven
anarchists to death. Had they read a word about what anarchism
was? Not one in a hundred, not one in a thousand; they simply knew
that these seven were *charged* with having thrown a bomb. That
was sufficient! This is the nature of American freedom. It demands
just the right degree of liberalism from the individual, no more, no
less. Toward those who overstep the bounds in any direction it is
as intolerant as a medieval despot. It is too conservative to budge one
step; today it remains standing where it stood two hundred years
ago. Time has not altered its forms one iota. For it is a democracy
fixed by law. If a writer turns up who believes in monarchy, this
writer is not free enough—the Americans run him out of the country; if a man emerges in that democratic mob who believes in anarchism as the eventual, most ideal form of society, this man is *too*
free—the Americans hang him! Whatever is more or less than
George Washington's exceedingly simple mind could grasp is punished by exile or loss of life. Such is American freedom—a freedom
not for the individual, the person, but freedom *en masse* and for all.

Recently the following notice appeared in *America*: "At last there
is some prospect that the heroes of the Haymarket are to receive a
lasting testimonial of their gallant conduct on that eventful May

night. The model of the Haymarket monument was recently completed by the sculptor [. . .] and will soon be sent to New York to be cast in bronze. The statue will be eight feet high [. . .] and will represent a patrolman defending the law, and is reported to be a remarkably artistic piece of work. It is about time that the efforts to obtain a suitable memorial [. . .] materialized, and, although no monument can represent the debt of gratitude the people of Chicago owe to the men who lost their lives in defense of the law, still it is well that the people are to have a memorial to remind them of that occasion."[2]

As for that occasion, however, the truth is this: in the first place it is the most recent major instance of American freedom, its nature and substance; it is also the most eloquent example of genuinely American legal proceedings. On May 4, 1886, an unseen hand threw a dynamite bomb at a large public gathering in Chicago's Haymarket Square, killing five policemen and injuring two.* No one knows who the perpetrator was; he may have been a cabman, a minister, or a congressman just as well as an anarchist. During the investigation—I mention this in passing—it was virtually ascertained that the authorities themselves had arranged to have a policeman throw the bomb in order, at a single stroke, to establish grounds for complaint against the leaders of the anarchists. But they simply took seven of the leading anarchists at random for these seven victims of the bomb. Five of the seven were condemned to death for the five that died as a result of the bomb, and two were sentenced to life imprisonment for the two who were only injured by the bomb. An eye for an eye! A tooth for a tooth! A practical and exceedingly American justice! One of the anarchists who was hanged, Parsons, was not even at the Haymarket the evening the bomb was thrown. "Well," they answered him, "but aren't you an anarchist?" "Yes!" said Parsons.[3]

This is the way those free Americans respond to ideas: they hang them. From the moment Editor Spies made public his shocking descriptions from the coal districts in Ohio, he was a dangerous man

---

* The others who were injured on the same occasion were immediately disregarded by the authorities.

who bore watching, a marked man foredoomed to death. And no sooner are the seven idealists cold in their nooses than the mob of freedom-loving Americans throughout Yankeeland raises a monument in memorial to the great patriotic deed of hanging ideas. And the newspapers thought it was about time it was done . . . . .

## II. Crime and the Judicial System

It is impossible to obtain a more comprehensive or truer illustration of social freedom and the American judicial system than the case of the anarchists. In all its revolting brutality, it characterizes to perfection the state of American society from top to bottom. It shows us a people that for the most part is made up of Europe's lowest types, going around and condemning to death the country's most intelligent men of ideas because they profess beliefs that the howling mob does not understand a syllable of. It shows us how the American courts, openly bribed and under the influence precisely of the demanding, ignorant mob, make the innocent take the blame for the guilty. Finally, it shows us which crimes are particularly frightening in that land of America—those crimes that do not occur every day, those that the mob is incapable of understanding—the crimes of *ideals*. The mere charge of political crimes was enough to fell these seven men, whereas crimes of a simpler, cruder, and therefore more readily understandable nature do not cause any stir. A murder committed in an entryway with the intent to rob, a congressman's unconcealed pillage in the national forests year after year, the cleverly devised land frauds of a railroad baron, the unprecedented bank swindles in New York of President Grant and his son-in-law—for such crimes it is possible in America to come to terms with the proper authorities on payment of a given assessment and in consonance with one's financial means. But the penalty for advocating social ideas in opposition to the despotic freedom of democracy is death.

It is indicative of the American judicial system that it is quite powerless when faced with fraud of any magnitude. Not because the country has no laws prohibiting fraud or because it is impossible to detect crimes over there, but because the courts can be bribed to an absolutely incredible extent. It is also indicative of the entire outlook of the American people, both their interests and their ways of thinking, that major frauds elicit their admiration, not to mention their sympathy. The ability to put over a smart swindle is regarded as an expression of Yankee ingenuity; the newspapers remark that it was very neatly done. Nor are the laws stringent in this respect; American criminal law is conceived in the "spirit of compromise." A couple of very recent happenings, chosen at random, will explain what I mean.

Six days before I left America the last time, a bank teller in New York stole $200,000 from his till. Was he apprehended? No. Where did he go? To Canada. Is he still there? He is still there. Last November 14, the owner of the Valparaiso Bank in Omaha disappeared; his name was Scoville. He made off with $300,000 more than was his, and he had managed it in the following manner: To the securities that were payable to his bank Scoville had appended certain additions—a practice that apparently occurs only in local American finance—so that the securities were now worth as much as twice their original value; thereafter Scoville deposited these securities in a couple of major banks that he was in the habit of drawing on and drew out the money. Then he disappeared. Where did he go? To Canada. Is he still there? He is still there. Canada is a safe place, a sanctuary; no scoundrel can be apprehended in Canada—there is no extradition agreement between Canada and the Union. Scoville is safe. After a train ride lasting a day and a night he found himself in a country where American criminal law could not reach him. What did the United States do now? The United States now did what it has always done on such occasions; it acted and operated in accordance with the "spirit of compromise." The United States sent a detective to Canada with instructions to negotiate with the swindler! If he turned over two thirds of his loot, Scoville would get to keep a third for himself. "And go free?" asked Scoville. "Come back and go free!" America answered its beloved son. Scoville was just about ready to go along with this, but then he had second thoughts. "I'll have to talk with my wife," says he. And the detective, who doubtless also has a wife, could readily understand that, when it was a question of $300,000 for a man, he had to talk with his wife. Accordingly Scoville talked with his wife. "No!" says his wife. And there was simply no mistaking that what she said was no. So that was the message the detective had to take back with him. Mrs. Scoville, who was almost the same as Mr. Scoville, had said no to America.

Now how was this business taken in the Union? It was shrugged off, forgotten for new swindles of the same kind, swindles toward which America acted in the very same fashion, in accordance with the very same "spirit of compromise." But the newspapers ran headlines about this splendid expression of the ingenious Yankee mind; they said a couple of times that it was neatly done, very neatly done. Then the whole thing died away.

Just as American laws are severe and inflexible when it comes to political crimes, so they are mild and indulgent when it comes to those brutal crimes, those simple peasant sins that every cunning prairie farmer is able to commit. An acquaintance of mine is the publisher of an anarchist paper—a paper the United States Post Office refuses to be contaminated by. The *Police Gazette*, published in New York, is the most contemptible sheet in the world, an organ almost exclusively devoted to the most shameless crimes in the Union: murder, adultery, rape, incest, fistfights, robberies, and swindles, often accompanied by lewd drawings printed on rose-colored paper—this sheet is handled by the United States Post Office. The *Police Gazette* has sixty thousand subscribers; it is found in hotels, barbershops, and clubs; it gets the Americans' undivided attention. It talks about crimes that everyone can understand—the simpleminded sins that any prairie farmer is able to commit with a brick.

When a foreigner starts digging into American crime statistics and attending American court sessions, he is astonished at how unusually crude and purposeless the crimes are in America. He gets the feeling increasingly that he is in a country that is not modern even in its crimes. In a hundred of one hundred and one instances, he looks in vain for some sign of sophistication, of, let us say, intelligence in these crimes; he finds that they do not resemble modern crimes so much as the misdoings he has read about from bygone ages. In America a great deal of cleverness is displayed in the implementation of a crime, but in most cases the purpose of the crime, its motive, its basis and idea, are simply proof of the brutish instincts of this backward people whom a disproportionate and inharmonious freedom is unable to control. Take a crime that is common to all countries—fraud, by which I mean forgery, a higher order of theft—forgery has quite a different character in America than in other countries (with certain exceptions here as elsewhere). Thus here at home forgery generally has its origin in a bad financial situation, but only in a very few instances does American forgery have its origin in a really critical financial situation—as everyone knows who has more or less kept up with the history of crime over there. No, forgery in America has its origin first and foremost in the Americans' insane craving for money salted away—even the smallest sum —that is, economic self-sufficiency, invincibility. A bank teller does not go off to Canada with the till because he is poorly paid; he gets a yearly salary of between 12,000 and 25,000 crowns. He goes off to Canada with the till because he cannot stand to look at the money he handles without possessing it himself, because his American blood prods him into stealing it, because *without* this money he is just an ordinary bank teller, because *with* this money he steps into the economic nobility—which is America's nobility. He is an American; he likes to throw money around, to be nicely dressed, to wear rings and gold trinkets, to eat at hotels, to be in demand in a small prairie town. This is the only ambition he has, and in order to satisfy this rather low-slung ambition he will stop at nothing; at last it drives him to forgery. There is nothing intelligent about his crime: he robs the till, takes a seat on the Erie express, rides a day and a night, and steps out in Canada as an American nobleman.

This cheap commonness characterizes all of America's crimes. Let a foreigner listen carefully to the sessions in an American city hall to see if he can find some hint of loftiness in the misdeed, let him really struggle to find even one element of refinement in the blue police reports—almost always he does so in vain. If one examines a nation's crimes as rationally as one examines the other phenomena of life, one is finally faced with the discovery that even in its crimes the

country is outdated and outdone. It is not even modern in its trans-
gressions. They are those committed by the Indians and the first
Dutch pioneers. People scalp the first man that comes along, they
blow up a bank in order to get pocket money for candy, they rip open
the stomach of five-year-old children and rape them, they rob a poor
devil of a daylaborer simply to lay hands on his money—every single
day the American newspapers are brimming over with accounts of
the brutish instincts that belong to this free people. American crimes
are even without formal elegance; sin in that country is characterized
by a gory shamelessness that has parallels only in the very distant
past; it is even without any elements of nobility or purpose. Such a
crime as the anarchists were accused of was bound to cause a commotion in such a country! And it did, too. Every well-bred hero who
knew his ABC's shouted "crucify!" Democratic old maids—of both
sexes—bought pictures of the anarchists and "hanged" them in their
windows. Shopkeepers advertised as follows: "Because we are *for* the
anarchists' being hanged, business is so good that we can afford to
sell our well-known blue Rio for nine cents a pound."

And not one in a hundred knew what anarchism was, not one in
a thousand. You see, it cannot automatically be assumed that the
Americans are the enlightened people we here at home go around
imagining them to be.

## III. Conditions in the Schools

It seems to me that it would be a positive miracle if the Americans
were an enlightened people. I am taking into consideration that the
Americans are a new nation made up of the most disparate and often
least enlightened people from other places, that it is made up of the
mentalities of every human race, the temperaments of every latitude;
I am taking into account that when considered as a nation the
Americans are in fact an artificial product, a mere experiment, instead of a result. I know that even the truest Yankee is but the son
of his father who again was but the son of a father whose grandfather was an immigrant thrall from Europe; I also know that 75
percent of America's current population consists of people, men and

women, whose parents fifty years ago became rootless in the Old World and whose children very definitely have not had time to put down roots in the New. And just crossing an ocean does not make one an educated man. This seems to be, however, what they in all seriousness would have us believe. At home in Norway, at any rate, the fact that a man has been in America has virtually meant that this man, then, knew more than his childhood prayers. If only he now has not gone and forgotten his childhood prayers! At birth even the truest Yankee still has a legacy from his immigrant forefathers; it is in his blood that he above and beyond all else must secure material well-being for himself—as it was the sole craving of the first immigrants to secure material well-being for themselves; it was for this reason alone that they came to the country. This dominant drive has been passed on to their progeny. Education, positive knowledge, learning—this just has to take care of itself until people can well afford it and, when people can well afford it, their desire to learn has long since passed. It would quite simply be contrary to the entire order of nature if the Americans were an enlightened people.

People have insisted on drawing the most sweeping conclusions from the fact that America has *free schools.* I am heartily convinced that the education obtained in these schools is in no way commensurate with their enormous expense. Why, even in the secondary schools both teachers and students are totally ignorant of the fact—to use an example already mentioned—that Norway had the telegraph in the year 1883, and in the primary schools they scarcely even know that there is a Norway; they know there is a Scandinavia, which in turn is Sweden. You grow very bitterly mistrustful of America's free schools after having observed their instruction for a while. You go there with the greatest expectations; you approach the place with fear and trembling. The schools are veritable palaces; the floors are so roomy and rambling that you almost need some knowledge of geography in order to find your way out again. Then you knock and step into the room—the entire class rises! This immediately makes the foreigner suspicious; he gets the feeling that the children are very much used to this performance. And this feeling does not lessen as the instruction goes on; even the teacher is taking account of the foreigner. He comes toward me smiling and offers me his hand;

he is "glad to see me" and wants to know where I come from. And then he gives a more or less detailed description—even in an English period and just on my account—of the "brave Scandinavians," their discovery of America, their industry, their ability to Americanize themselves, their participation in the Civil War. I learn of the most remarkable kings we supposedly have had at some time, of great sportsmen and bishops whose names I have never heard before, of the city of Spitzbergen where the people go around in seal skins, of such quantities of fish that we had to pray to heaven for deliverance, of mountains that could make a bald man's hair stand on end. I am also told of the skater Aksel Paulsen. This man, in fact, is the best-known Norwegian in America; his feet have made him into a big man—his picture has appeared in the *Police Gazette*. If as a Scandinavian you want to uphold the honor and glory of your nationality in America, then speak, saying that you are a countryman of Aksel Paulsen. If in one way or another you can make yourself a cousin of this man, it is not impossible that the Americans will give a party for you.

It is a mixed pleasure to sit listening to the instruction in the American free schools. The instruction is not a systematic working through of the subject under consideration; it is primarily intended as *entertainment* for the pupils, in which there is but a sprinkling of positive knowledge. However admirable an instructional method may be that puts such emphasis on interesting the pupils and making school attractive to them, it nevertheless has the disadvantage of easily becoming abstract. It drifts onto everything under the sun, now and then turning into pure amusement; it makes use of jokes and tells stories—in which at times there is a sprinkling of positive knowledge. The teacher is an American, a born orator, a speech-maker who tosses out odds and ends of knowledge to the school benches, inquiring constantly whether the pupils have understood him and entreating them not to forget what he has just said. A period, which according to the schedule is assigned to one thing, can very easily turn into a period for absolutely anything. In visiting a school one Saturday, I choose in advance a period that is set aside for "rhetoric"; I want to listen to American rhetoric. Now I am wise from experience; in answer to the teacher's inquiry about where I am from, I make myself into a German without blinking an eye. But I have done so without thinking. Unfortunately the spirit comes over him; he is rhetorically disposed. The upshot is a lecture about everything under the sun that drifts onto the subject of Germany. Yet in every comment there is a piece of isolated information, more or less factual, about one thing or another, forming an interesting conglomeration of information from schoolbooks and knowledge gained from newspapers, lexicons, and sunday-school magazines. The speech is always severely moral, not to mention religious; instruction in these "nonconfessional" schools is conducted in the very same spirit of religious orthodoxy as in our common schools.*[4] Even when in the course of the hour the teacher—the speaker—gets into European conditions and talks about free thought, anarchism, and every other kind of social ruination, he always tries to draw the proper moral from these things; thus with the right spirit even Count Bismarck can become a Republican and Voltaire an archbishop in Budapest. A fact more or less is of lesser import than a moral that is a matter of fact. Before I left this period in rhetoric I had learned that the first living-room clock was invented in Germany in 1477—which I believe was true—and that Ferdinand Lassalle died converted to Christianity in 1864—which I believe was a lie.

Without any doubt, one gets a more thorough education in certain subjects in the American common schools than in the grade schools here at home. I can mention such examples as arithmetic, mapmaking, penmanship, American history and geography, and declamation. I also admit that my general knowledge of the American educational system is sorely inadequate. Possibly I have not even attended every subject; in any event I have obviously not visited every school. I have simply taken an interest in this matter because school instruction in America—as everywhere else—is the initial seedbed for the country's cultural and intellectual life. I have questioned pupils, I have talked to teachers of both sexes, I have seen the most essential of the school materials, and I am now heartily convinced that the American free schools cost more than they are worth. An unmerci-

* See Professor Rovsing's book on American schools, about which he says: "Patriotism and religion belong in all of them" (p. 10).

ful number of subjects are taught so that both declamation and rhetoric, yes, even "philosophy," are included in the class schedule, but
it has struck me that this wholesale learning operates more in breadth
than in depth. In all my contact with Americans—and I have had
not a little contact with them in the course of several years and various occupations—I have never noticed, for example, that the philosophy they learned in school has ever penetrated very deeply. And
were I to draw a parallel with another country, I would, in order
not to mention Norway, mention Ireland. I have never met children
or adults in Ireland that were less enlightened than in America, not
even in the heart of Ireland. However, my main complaint against
the American free schools is that they teach the children absolutely
nothing about foreign peoples and foreign customs, about the modern cultures of Europe and Asia, about the world. One gets the impression that the American schools are much too patriotic to instruct
their pupils in world history. Only on special occasions, when there
is a visitor, does it happen that the teacher has a fit of general historical knowledge; he gives a lecture, he talks about everything under
the sun, racing through all the cultural epochs and mentioning
Moses, Napoleon, and Aksel Paulsen.

Now what is the relationship between the cost of these free schools
in America and the instruction they provide? What do America's
free schools cost? I call your attention to the fact that this word
"free" is to be understood as free of charge, that is, *free* schools mean
schools that are *free of charge*. These schools that are free of charge
in America are perhaps the most expensive schools in the world. But
people speak in such glowing terms about these schools just because
they are "free of charge." When an American wants to point out to
a foreigner what grand advantages his country has over all other
countries, he of course mentions political freedom first of all—but
thereafter the free, that is, gratis schools. If a foreigner comes to a
strange town and buys a city guide, he finds these free, that is,
gratis schools among the sights to see in the town. For these gratis
schools, however, America pays in the neighborhood of two hundred
million dollars annually. This is absolutely one of the most mon-
strous items of expenditure in the country. It still does not include

expenditures for Sunday schools—an expense that is growing by leaps and bounds as the country becomes more and more Catholic. Now, it is far from accurate to call these schools gratis. They are no more gratis than the public schools in every other country. When therefore the newspapers here at home and the Yankees in America wish to prove that these schools are gratis, they start with the erroneous premise that in America only those people with means pay school taxes; poor people can send their children to school without paying anything. This way of looking at it does not go deep enough. As if the poorest, the most destitute father in town does not pay school taxes! He pays taxes whenever he buys a pound of meat from a cart, since you see he is paying for the butcher's license; he pays school taxes whenever he turns on his gaslight at night, whenever he drinks a glass of water; he pays school taxes whenever he walks where there are electric streetlights. But, say the newspapers here at home and the Yankees in America, the taxes for water come under another heading in the bookkeeping, another budget. This is simply something that can be said, not proven, not defended. Every American city—as well as every rural township—has its own treasury. This treasury is filled by the taxpayers, whose taxes constitute payment for all the grand things the city has provided them with as residents, and it is emptied by the city's administration for the public weal or woe. Now, the city is the state in miniature, and the state is a complex of relationships. When the individual with means incurs large expenses for schools, the individual with lesser means is taxed in sectors whose cost would otherwise have been borne exclusively by the individual with more means if he had not had the expenses for schools. Taxes are determined on the basis of assets, income; so much for one individual *because* he is rich but also so much for you *in spite of* your being poor. And you do pay school taxes.

In order to get a better idea of the actual immensity of American school taxes, you can compare the school budget of one of our cities with the school budget of a comparable city in America. Copenhagen has set aside 1,300,000 crowns for schools; Minneapolis—the city the size of Copenhagen—has 3,300,000 crowns or exactly two million crowns more. This still does not include expenditures for church schools. But the benefits derived from the American schools do not in any way seem commensurate with the lavish provision for their operations. As adults the pupils of these schools sit at the atheneum and read patent reports and detective stories to their soul's delight, and in spite of all the "philosophy" they once heard from the lips of their teachers, they still refer a foreigner who asks for Hartmann to the American, Pastor Emerson.

I repeat that the American people never show any evidence of their monstrously expensive school system's having produced any special fruits of mind or spirit; you will find that they reflect a minimum of education, which in the majority of subjects amounts to sheer ignorance. The fact, on the other hand, that they are ahead of us in several other subjects, notably arithmetic and national history, has not unequivocally given rise to the most intelligent features in the Americans as a people. Their superfluous knowledge of the slightest detail in the history of their own country—for example, their eternal reading of America's famous military exploits —has perhaps helped not a little to bolster the nation's smugness, making the Yankees even more patriotic than they were before. And when it comes to their proficiency in arithmetic, this proficiency, if it has not encouraged, certainly has not moderated either their vulgar miserliness or their innate desire to grapple with material values. A Yankee boy is not very old before he tries to cheat a streetcar conductor out of a ticket, and when he is a grown man and there is an election, he openly sells his vote for so many dollars and so many cents.

## IV. Morality and the Churches

Theological studies at American universities take three years. It is worth noting that in comparison medical studies take only a year at most—at several universities even as little as four months.* The fact that there are medical students who take additional training and that there are also distinguished medical men in America (Thomas, Adams, etc.) still does not stop a man with four months of medical study from going out and practicing his ignorance on his

* See Official Report of the Illinois State Board of Health, 1888.

countrymen. Secretary of the Board Rauch has fought earnestly against this medical swindle, but to no avail. He has been unable to either check or stamp out the innumerable "medical colleges" springing up alongside the medical colleges and the swarms of "professors" multiplying around the professors; great is the power of humbug in America. "Here and there, naturally, one comes across capable doctors, intelligent students, well-equipped schools that are the exception; but the status of medical instruction in America is disgracefully low . . . European institutions of the same kind are far and away superior to our own because they are older; and however much can be said against monarchies (!), they do encourage medical science. There a professorship in this field is generally a reward for merit, for competence, learning, whereas in our chairs of medicine we find a preponderance of scrambling medical politicians, mediocrities, and just plain ignoramuses whose 'medical' lectures consist of bragging, guesswork, religious platitudes, and medical jargon" (*America*).[5]

Here, one year is to three years as time is to eternity: one year to learn how to save men from death on earth, three years to learn how to preach eternal life. Or more accurately: one year to learn how to save people for life on earth, three years to learn how to give advance warning of—eternal death. *Honi soit, qui mal y pense!*

In America the churches are livelier, more active than one would ever imagine. In reality, religious propagandizing is so diligently pursued in this country where materialism flourishes preeminently—whether unbeknownst to this materialism, so to speak, or in retaliation for it—that the situation may well be compared to the English and their worship of tea. America is a rich country; there is money for everything and anything. The blackest Negro or most sinful Zulu kaffir is not too expensive for the American capitalist infected with the desire to proselytize. America is a rich country! There are so many ministers and churches and guardians of morality and Lutheran foundations and the White Cross and youth organizations and all kinds of virtuous endeavors that people in poorer countries can but imagine them in their mind's eye. And even so, is freedom so ignoble, the judicial system so corrupt, the crimes so barbaric? Even so!

For the sake of clarity—yet another parallel. When one counts all the religious meetinghouses and chapels, indeed, even the Bethel ship, Copenhagen has 29 churches. But when one has counted all the churches, large and small, in Minneapolis—the city the size of Copenhagen—Minneapolis has 146 churches. There is a great deal of God in America! The churches are very richly furnished, magnificently furnished; in Minneapolis there is thus a church to which a rich man has donated a window worth five hundred dollars. There is a subdued, pleasing light that filters in through the multicolored glass; there are deep, soft seats, immense organs, rugs on the floor, polished doors, polished people, polished Scripture. In rainy weather it is really very pleasant to attend divine worship in an American church. The sermon, you see, is neither Norwegian, Swedish, nor Danish; it is American. It does not contain theology but morality, Boston morality, adapted to the tolerances of people in silk. The sermon is a thoroughly interesting lecture, interspersed with humor that the entire congregation is not afraid to laugh at boisterously—in all propriety. As a rule you do not learn a thing from these sermons; in this they resemble the sermons here at home. But they possess a certain logic, human language, illustrative stories, and in this they do not always resemble the sermons here at home. Thus they do not develop the mind, though they are entertaining. And in that they have merit. Many a time in America I have preferred personally— even with a free theater pass in my pocket—to go to church in the evening rather than to the goings-on at a theater. Whereas the theaters had only debased art, half art, nonart to offer, the churches offered a lecture whose language at any rate was very agreeable; moreover there was no risk of suffocating from the gunsmoke or being hit in the head with cigar butts. And all those people who went to church were now, after all, the most respectable people in town, handsome people whom it was a joy to behold. In passing let it be said that the Americans are an extremely handsome stock. All in all it would be hard to find handsomer people in any other country. Sometimes you meet pigheaded lieutenants here at home who ask if the Americans' eternal concern with money matters, with calculating and speculating—if, after all, such things have not coarsened their appearance. Perhaps. Very little is known of the original

American type—the one initiated by the first immigrants; there is very little opportunity to compare and thus see to what extent the Yankees now have fallen off physically. As it is, they are simply handsome people with well-formed bodies and healthy, energetic faces. Among other things, their eyes are in good shape, which is more than can be said of Europeans. In Europe glasses constitute a piece of wearing apparel, but in America you very rarely run across a person with glasses. If you now and again encounter bespectacled people down East, they are most generally Negroes. These Negroes have presumably studied a bit at some school, and it was more than they could tolerate, studying a bit at some school.

Americans are diligent churchgoers. The majority of those going to church are of course women, but a number of men are also politic enough to go there. It is quite imperative for a Yankee, if he wants to get ahead in the world, to be in good standing with the churches; indifference to the church and her upper and lower regions, that is, her heavenly and temporal affairs (which again means just the temporal), is an indifference that is punished unconditionally. When a manufacturer donates bricks for the repair of a cracked wall, his name is solemnly mentioned in the following Sunday's sermon, and the thanks he receives for those bricks come virtually straight from God. When, on the other hand, another manufacturer does not even send twenty-odd men to get the wall back into shape, then *his* name is very definitely not mentioned in the sermon. The majority of Americans are smart enough to understand the impact of an advertisement made through the church. And they avail themselves of it. No Yankee likes to have to refuse a minister anything; it pays to help him. The shopkeepers give him a 10 percent discount *because* he is a minister; similarly, the railroad companies sell him his ticket at half price *because* he is a minister. When a minister goes to an employer seeking work for a man, the employer is smart enough not to refuse him if in any way he can help it; he prefers not to, even if he does not have any openings. It is then also important for this worker to try to stay on friendly terms with the minister's church. This interchange of mutual help and support, of bricks and the Word of God, makes American churches rather worldly—which just suits the country's materialistic temper. It gives help only to the extent that it is itself helped. It lays great stress on fine furnishings, and the good soul who donates a chandelier or gold-embroidered alms receptacle in green silk containing a small, genuine diamond—that good soul will not have done so in vain. The lumber dealer who has kept a pretty close eye on the church's temporal requirements, that is, the wants and needs of what I will again call her lower regions—that lumber dealer gets customers; he does business.

With each passing year the ministers in America grow more and more powerful; Catholicism especially is sweeping triumphantly over the land, and in time it may not leave a stone standing. In this connection it is informative to know that Minneapolis, which after all is a somewhat Scandinavian city, has a total of twenty-one large Catholic institutions while the remaining denominations together have only two. When traveling down through the East by rail, you pass towns that are completely Catholic. You see churches, large schools, universities, children's homes, huge convents—the entire town is Catholic. Nor does the Catholic Church in America lack money; for the most part it gets its recruits from the Irish, who are the largest ethnic group in the country, and the Irish almost always do well over there. They have just the right kind of agility for wriggling into all of life's possibilities.

The very fact that ministers are hired before elections to travel about campaigning for this candidate or that, the very fact that ministers are thus preferred as political agitators shows how much more authority ministers have in this area, too, than those far better acquainted with the country's politics. Here too the Yankee has a legacy from his immigrant forefathers. "Thy God shall be my God; naught but death shall part us." It is no longer implicit faith that moves the great masses of people to follow their ministers; next to the material advantages involved, they are driven to it by a precept of tradition, a kind of congenital religiosity. In the Americans religious faith has acquired an aspect which makes it distinctive; it has become a faith which our native theologians would probably call by the readily understood term "habitual faith" but which might be more accurately designated by such a term as "faith by inheritance," "faith-ism." People believe because people have believed, because people's belief has gone into their flesh and blood through many, many generations. Therefore people believe not implicitly but matter-of-factly. You also get this impression of faith-ism in the Americans when attending their churches. It was reassuring for the foreign sinner to observe the calm and sedate manner in which they worshiped their God. They entered the church as if they were coming to any ordinary lecture, found places, sat down in the soft, deep seats, leaned back and listened—while the minister stood there for a blessed hour worrying about the salvation of their souls. No tears, no histrionics such as an implicit faith might have elicited; on the other hand, no indifference. The whole thing seemed to be meant seriously, as something midway between contrition and exultation, bricks and the Word of God, in short, regular faith-ism. This faith-ism can be so alive that it never occurs to a foreigner that it is dead; but then it has to be the real thing, the only true species of Yankee faith-ism, so to speak. With the Yankees it is genuine, genuine and alive. It does not manifest itself in histrionics but in a modulated pleasure, interestedness. If you remain in America for awhile, little by little you come to understand that for great numbers of Yankees the Lord is just about as popular as George Washington— and that can be a good thing for the Lord!

But the high incidence of church attendance in America is not an infallible index of the Americans' high morality. There are many good Americans who commit the blackest deeds on Saturday and yet go to church the next day. Even a Yankee is human and human beings are alike everywhere. You do not get the feeling that American ministers, with all their authority, have managed to engender any great moral sense in their congregations. The state of America's morality is most accurately gauged by observing its freedoms, judicial system, and crimes; and the fruits of this morality scarcely tolerate display.

America's morality is money.

Here at home people have spoken very highly of religious freedom in America. In reality there is not so much of it as we are accustomed to assuming. Here, as always in that country of America, money comes first. If a man is rich, he can of course keep a horse and carriage instead of a minister, and no one criticizes him for it. But if a man is poor, he must not even keep bread on his table before keeping a minister. People simply do not take to a poor man's doing without a minister. America's morality is money.

There is a man in America by the name of Ingersoll. He is free to descend upon American cities with something people call lectures on free thought. I will not on the contrary call these lectures free of thought, but I will say that there is indeed very little thinking in the lectures of that man. Ingersoll, however, travels up and down America preaching godlessness for a dollar a ticket. No one hinders him in this traffic. On the contrary. A train conductor with Ingersoll on board feels that for once in his life he is traveling with a great man. And when Ingersoll steps off the train, he can immediately read of his arrival in an extra edition of the town's largest paper. For Ingersoll is a colonel from the war, which is to say a patriot; a lawyer, which is to say a good talker; and a rich man, which says it all. He is the owner of immense estates.

There is another man by the name of Bennett; compared to Ingersoll he is a very intelligent man, this Bennett, editor of *The Truth-seeker*, author of two large volumes of comparative religion in addition to numerous tracts of varying length. This man has been in American prisons for his free thinking. Why has he been in prison for his free thinking? Because he was not a colonel (patriot), not a lawyer (good talker), and because he was a poor man. In one of his pamphlets he had had something special to say about the religious humbug of Americans; that was going too far—Ingersoll had never done that. When Ingersoll had something special to say about Americans, he says it about the Old Testament; he never points out any special failings in his own countrymen, never finds a dangerous cloud in the American sky. He is the most insipid patriot in his homeland. But Bennett went to prison. It is a fact that the man was too poor to save himself from prison.[6]

There is a third man, Pearl Johnson. He had the absolutely insane idea that some people were really pretty polygamous creatures; he wrote a book in which he defended a rather free kind of love—to prison with him! He was exclusively a theorist, poor man; he lived in a garret in New York and apparently did not even know any other woman by name than his own mother, but he had to go to prison. He was too poor to hire a lawyer.[7]

America's morality is money.

As a contrast to this last example of morality and the way in which it manifests itself in America, it is interesting to observe how that same morality manifests itself in the same country with respect to *women*.

The predominance women have in America is more accurately described as domination. When they are out walking on the street, they have—regardless of right of way—a right to the inside of the walk; if twelve men and one woman are in an elevator at the same time, the twelve men have to stand bareheaded while riding up and down in deference to this one woman; if a streetcar has fifty passengers and a woman steps aboard, a man has to rise and give her his seat; if a woman is a witness in court, her testimony is equal to that of two men; if a man, out of carelessness, swears in the presence of a woman, he must immediately beg her forgiveness. On American farms it is always the man who gets up first in the morning; only after he has lighted the stove, put water on to boil, and milked the cows out in the barn, only then does he waken his wife. A man who has a wife can prosecute a Chinaman who has a laundry because the Chinaman hangs up underpants to dry in a spot where the man's wife can catch sight of them. A woman who may even make her living off good men can easily get a picture of a small nude shepherd by Correggio confiscated right from the owner's bedroom: a verdict in Chicago two years ago proves it. If therefore—to transfer the situation—if therefore a horse standing on Karl Johan Street winked at a woman cashier in Pascha's bookstore, that cashier, if she were an American, could just give a policeman a wink, whereupon that policeman, if he were an American, would immediately impound the horse . . . . . In America a woman can get away with things that are actually not allowed. Unlike Pearl Johnson, for instance, who merely preached free love and was punished, the American woman *practices* free love and goes free. A man takes a train trip, he disappears, he sends no word; three or four months later the grief-stricken "widow" goes to the judge and says as follows: "I should like to ask for a divorce," says she. "My husband took a train trip and since then he has not been home," she says. Pale with compassion the judge replies: "What a husband! He has not been home all this time!" And then afterward he asks—just as a minor formality: "How long has it been?" "Three months," answers the "widow" with her last ounce of strength. "Divorce granted!" cries the judge, and the "widow" is divorced.

You have only to read the newspapers for a while to find evidence of how much easier it is for a woman to get a divorce in America than a man. In the larger cities the Saturday edition of every newspaper has a special page for divorces. They appear there in the form of courtroom accounts and always end with the same refrain: "Divorce granted!" But the great majority of divorces occur at the request of the woman in the suit. The very fact that a man has been away for three or four months without sending any money home is enough to deprive him of his wife; incidentally, these divorces are simply up to the judge, since everything depends on his sympathies in the case.

It is in the churches, as you would expect, that you encounter that segment of American women who have had the fewest divorces in their lives and who consequently reflect the very best breeding in town. Respectable people, handsome people whom it is an aesthetic pleasure to behold. Why are they sitting here? Scarcely for the immediate purpose of initiating and strengthening the very highest moral sense. Even American women are human, and human beings are very much alike everywhere. They sit here in virtue of their faith-ism. They are interested in hearing what may be said on God's behalf against the latest happenings out on the prairie or in town, all of which the minister explains in his lecture. He includes every smit and smidgeon; he documents his statements with newspaper clippings, with rumors he has wrung from an editor's locals, with the private reports of men who knew all the details about one current issue or another. "A friend of mine told me one day recently," he says, and then he relates what that friend of his has told him one day recently. Then the women in the congregation prick up their ears. For coming now is either a piece of news or something funny. And both are worth pricking up one's ears for—in all propriety.

What is there otherwise that makes American women such diligent churchgoers? Next to faith-ism it is the fact that they are not neglecting anything in doing so. They have time for this religious entertainment; they have nothing to do. Truly American women have no house to manage, no husband to help, no children to raise; in the first two years of marriage they may have as many as two children—through carelessness; then they have no more. Sitting there now at the youthful age of thirty to thirty-five, they no longer have any children to look after. They have absolutely nothing to look after; they are unemployed persons. Their cares consist of tending their nerves in the morning, painting works of art until two o'clock, reading *Uncle Tom's Cabin* until six o'clock, and taking a stroll until eight o'clock. The schedule of their daily activities is variable, however. Three or four times a week they may feel impelled —in spite of the great artistic burdens weighing upon them—to steal a modest eight to eleven hours daily for participation in women's congresses. This cannot be neglected either; heaven knows how extremely essential it is!

So American women find they are capable of the following occupations in this world: suffering from nerves, painting works of art, enjoying Negro poetry, strolling and participating in congresses. On the other hand, they do not find time to have children. By bringing two paper hens into the world they feel that they have fulfilled their maternal mission. In a way they want to avoid having children; they do not want the bother of nursing them; it is too much trouble. As a result all the Yankees' ingenuity is set in motion, looking for means of preventing childbirth. American women are as thoroughly familiar with these measures as ours are with Luther's catechism. If things nevertheless go wrong in spite of these measures—through carelessness—there is still a remedy: in the same country where a man in the name of morality is condemned to prison for a theory of free love, doctors openly advertise their specialty in abortion. And no one gets after them for it. On the contrary, they have clients; American women come to them. If it now happens that things still do not go as desired—one can of course go to the doctor a small matter of four or five months too late—then misfortune has to run its course. A veritable child is born, to put it bluntly, an audaciously real child. And that is a misfortune. No chairmanship in a women's congress accompanies such a child. And this the mother rues. Meanwhile she will not nurse the child; rather than be plagued with nursing it, she has her husband go out to the barn and get cow's milk. Fifty percent of the annual mortality rate in the United States is comprised of children under the age of five. Along with several of his colleagues, Dr. De Wolff, medical director of one of the largest hospitals in the Union (Chicago's), has declared publicly that the major cause of the unreasonably high mortality rate among children can be sought exclusively in American mothers' distaste for breast-feeding. Of one hundred live births in America, forty infants die before the age of one. (As I recall, the figure is ten in Norway.) Glass factories in the United States have an annual production of over ten million nursing bottles. The day the Yankees completely shut their gates to emigrants, they are going to have to hire the few Indian women that are left in order to maintain their population . . . . .

The way American women now sit in church, thirty to thirty-five years old, beautiful, well-bred women whom it is an aesthetic pleasure to behold, they may just have a small account to settle with their heavenly Washington. And they do so with absolute composure. These people do not rise above the common level of morality in America, but neither do they violate that morality. And that is the main thing.

## V. ETIQUETTE

Social practices in America are ostensibly the same as those encountered in England; in the large eastern cities of America especially, etiquette bears the greatest formal resemblance to the English. In the social world English amusements, English hospitality, and

English sports are the height of fashion. Horse racing, dog fights, boxing, hunting, ball games, and cricket have become the most popular and fashionable outdoor sports; the cults of tea drinking and missions, beef, respectability, and discussions of mining and railroad speculations are the favorite indoor intellectual diversions of the "salons." The dude in New York can hold his own against his London counterpart both in white linen and yellow topcoats as well as in anemic gray matter, and the married women in the wealthy homes of Boston are scarcely to be outdone by any English lady, either in guiding their persons across the floor to a chair or in tactfully guiding a conversation to a standstill. The majority of people, particularly in the western towns of America, make fun of the English for their sideburns, their ancient queen, and especially their English; but in reality every American has the utmost respect for England and adopts with reverence whatever the English emigrants bring to Yankeeland of pure, unadulterated British etiquette. If you go to Washington you will find this more evident than anywhere else in America. Here, among society people both young and old, English attitudes and manners prevail. Often the daughter of a rich Washingtonian's wife seems directly imbued with traces of the English legation secretary's British manner: she shows the proper degree of elegant indolence in her bearing, a suitable phlegmatism in her speech, and she lisps quite admirably. The fact, on the other hand, that such a lady may go running off to Canada with her father's most irresistible Negro stableboy is assuredly true, but this must be regarded as an instance of atavism, as a small, unconscious recurrence of the old Adam, of one's Yankee nature, which is too strong to resist.[8]

What makes American etiquette national, thereby differentiating it from the English, is thus quite literally its Yankee nature; despite all its outward resemblance to England's, it is still fundamentally American. The English are aristocrats, the Americans democrats—precisely these varying instincts basic to the two peoples determine their differing customs and give character to their etiquette. You have a sense of this disparity in manners even between the inhabitants of the American Union and English Canada. When you travel by train, alternately spending the night in American and Canadian hotels, you immediately seem to detect a more respectful greeting, a more intelligent answer from the Canadians than the Americans. It takes very little to bring out this difference. The faintest trace of sincerity when a chair is offered, the slightly less venial manner in which a bill is presented, are things that immediately appeal to your sensibilities and impress you as expressions of an at once different and more cultivated mind. American minds are without aristocratic qualities; they are thoroughly democratized; they are trained to be alike, standardized in their perceptions, used to expressing themselves without nobility. In a word, they are without plasticity of thought or feeling. A Yankee can learn all the features of English good manners by heart; he can have the rules of etiquette at his fingertips, but inside he is nevertheless the same old prairie dweller. He will never become an aristocrat in temperament. The Englishman has a tradition, a heritage of cultural nobility, whose elements are in his blood; the American on the other hand is a man of today, an upstart, self-taught in background and social behavior. He reminds one of a man with a distinguished forename and exceedingly democratic surname—let us say Ørnstjerne Olsen. However high his eagle-like Ørnstjerne may soar in English polish, his Olsen drags him back down to his fundamental national character, that of a Negro stableboy.

There is so little of the aristocrat in Americans that even their late, celebrated war was in reality a struggle against the aristocracy. It was perhaps not so much a war for morality[*9] or for emancipation of the Negroes as for extermination of the Southern aristocracy. After all, the notion that an entire people—and the American people at that—can become enraged out of a sense of morality is a trifle naive. That smacks of Boston; it sounds like the feminist movement. If the Yankees really fought against the South for the sake of morality, then why for the last quarter of a century since then have the Yankees tolerated overt immorality as the exclusive form of social organization in Utah, which lies smack in the heart of America?

* See Bjørnson's "Engifte og mangegifte," p. 14.

The war was christened the War against Slavery. Why not? A war has to have one Christian motive or another—an official name; so it is called the War against Slavery. But talk to the officers and men in that war, ask them what above all got them to fight, what it was that set them on fire, and you will get an answer from those officers and men that deviates sharply from all the memoirs of Grant and others like him. When a Yankee colonel gives a speech on Decoration Day, he speaks from beginning to end on democracy's triumph over the "damned aristocracy"; when a General Logan dies, the American press urges his widow to write a book about this democrat's triumph over the "damned Southern aristocrats." Ask the veterans from the Northern states what it was that prompted them to murder Southern women, burn plantations in Missouri, suffocate old people with hot ashes, drive rusty nails through the skulls of Southern hogs, gouge the flanks of horses and cows belonging to the Southern plantation owners with their sabers and pour petroleum into the wounds—ask the officers and men if all this was done out of a sense of moral decency and in order to free the slaves! The war was a war against the aristocracy, waged with all the democrat's ferocious hatred of the plantation nobility in the South. The very same Northern states—the morally decent Northern states—that at the time wanted to crush the aristocracy in the South were themselves speculating in slavery. This the good women of Boston forget. Capitalists in the Northern states had immense landholdings in the South; when the war broke out, the Southern plantation owners owed enormous sums to the North. It was common practice for capitalists in the East to give the Southern planters a cash advance on the year's crops, an advance secured by mortgages on the plantation itself and the Negroes. How is that for moral decency! How is that for zealous devotion to the freeing of Uncle Tom!

That American thinking expresses itself so correctly in formal terms and yet is so totally lacking in intrinsic nobility, in the poetry of the soul—this leaves its mark on etiquette as well. It is without sincerity; it is shorn of all symbolic value. When without reservation Americans prefer to attend a match between two recognized boxers rather than see Sarah Bernhardt in *Ruy Blas*, then this same lack of intellectual preoccupation is repeated in every aspect of their training and social behavior: this useless inanity pervades their greetings, their dress, the climate of their social life, even the street life of their large cities. If one evening, as you are walking along the most fashionable street in an American town, you select a strolling couple whom you then follow closely while listening unobserved to their conversation, you will get a very accurate idea of the prevailing tone in American social intercourse. If you repeat this experiment every evening for some time, always making certain to find a new couple, your impression from the last conversation will be exactly the same as from the first, inasmuch as both sprang from the same nonintellectual outlook on life and revolved around the same major topics: business, fights, sports, weather conditions, family affairs, train accidents, arrests. The couple may be engaged—that does not alter the nature of their conversation. The woman is wearing silk, which is a very typical costume in the country; her taste is revealed in the most absurd color combinations—black, blue, white, and red buttons on the same bodice; an orange scarf at one hip; streamers of gilded ribbon; rosettes placed without rhyme or reason. American women adorn themselves brilliantly—even Solomon was not arrayed like one of these! The couple is typical. As the lady loves the wildest transitions from dark to the most piercing light, so that she can completely destroy the inherent good sense of her costume by sheer color, so the gentleman's suit also displays the same old disharmony, without which it would not be an American suit. A Yankee buys a hat for ten to fifteen dollars, but he may very well go around in a pair of trousers that has buttons missing in a spot where a pair of trousers must not have buttons missing. He is Ørnstjerne of hat and Olsen of pants. In the hot weather you must not ask for coat and vest on the frame of a true Yankee; strolling through the streets with a woman, he is just as much at ease without this apparel as with it.

During the day the streets of an American city quiver with feverish restlessness. Businessmen in hurried strides work their way to and from the bank, to and from the wholesale houses, to and from their customers; the empty streetcars go rolling off behind the broken-down mules; the women sit in "congress" and debate Dakota's transition from territory to statehood; the promising son goes off to the atheneum and reads patent reports; the reporter stands on the street corner, his ears alert to news of a fire or fight for the morning edition; but the professional dandy, the dude, with his high starched collar and gold-headed cane is sitting in his shirt sleeves in a well-protected spot, cheating a farmer at gambling.

Toward evening the street changes character; at six o'clock the city promenades. And every living creature in the entire town comes creeping forth; the banks close, the atheneum locks up its treasures for the night, the ladies are out swinging their lieutenants the way a lieutenant is supposed to be swung; but the professional dandy has done his deed, having cleaned out the slow-witted farmer the way a farmer is supposed to be cleaned out. And the broken-down mules drag the loaded streetcars through the streets and the saloons fill up with thirsty Germans of every nation and the factories close their great iron-mounted doors and swarms of blackened working-men, their dented lunch pails in hand, swing into the side streets, and the paperboy barks out news of a juicy murder in Kansas City! Now the dude's big moment has arrived; he has been waiting for this hour all day. The first silk dress to appear on Nicollet Avenue puts him right in the mood. To go around eyeing the latest cut in jackets, getting into loud discussions about the most recent nose-battering antics of two boxers, making wisecracks in the current lingo, flinging cynical gibes at the poor sinners from the back rooms —these are his life's interests. There are gifted people among these dudes, handsome people, quick-witted, shrewd Yankees, Americans with Irish blood, young gentlemen who live at fine restaurants during the day and sleep on a chair in a saloon at night, derelicts and gentlemen, kept paramours who await the Misses Railey outside the church on warm evenings and accept two dollars in cash— to help a neighbor in bodily need . . . . .

One's chief impression of American street life is the people's general lack of intellectual preoccupation. That fecund air of inanity in which the Yankees live is just right for producing dudes with anemic brains. Neither art nor books are to be seen in the shop-windows; one is therefore compelled to stare at the carved Indians outside the cigar stores. If gentlemen or ladies walk along the street reading the latest paper, they are reading about murders and calamities. If an engaged couple walks along conversing about the things closest to their hearts, they are talking about business and the weather. At the same time, all the strollers keep a sharp eye out for the slightest break in the traffic—an intoxicated woman, an overloaded streetcar, a man with glasses.

One day four hundred people had gathered in the square near Scandia Bank. What were these people doing there? They were standing there looking at a load of stones that had become stuck in the streetcar tracks. And in the houses round about there were clusters of faces in every window, both young and old faces, filled with excitement as they viewed the miracle; people came galloping from adjacent streets, people right down to old crones came galloping in order to look at this load of stones. I have yet to experience anything like it in any country where I have traveled; that entire mob of people stood there looking at that load of stones as if it were a drama of world importance. Now people are going to say that it was just a mob—youth, a mob. But not predominantly. They were Americans. There were notable men from the city among them, women from the "congress," fashionable people. It was a mob in furs, women in expensive costumes, a mob in silk; it was a mob that could have afforded to wear the large Odd Fellows' badge on their chests, a mob with twenty dollars' worth of gold in their mouths alone. They were Americans.

The last winter that I was in America I had an experience with a pair of snow leggings that in all had twenty-two buttons. Now I will admit that there were perhaps one or two buttons too many on those leggings—yes, I will admit that; but still there was only one button for each buttonhole, and you will have to grant that to a legging. But the good citizens of that big city could not in all conscience keep from staring at those leggings. When I had the nerve to go down the main street of the city, every eye in the head of every true Yankee was following me, and it seemed to me that I had never seen so many people on the streets as on the days when I was wearing those leggings. Had I been a strolling theater, I could not have created a greater sensation, and I was not at all certain but that I might get an offer to appear at some vaudeville theater. At last the attention I was attracting with my leggings began to get a bit ticklish. Even the police stood there looking at them, pondering whether they could avoid arresting those leggings. The upshot was that I gave them away—I really did—I gave them to my worst enemy, a lumberjack from Texas, with whom I thus settled accounts on very amicable terms.

But such trivia can engross Americans, such bagatelles as two buttons too many on a legging—such things as what a person has on his legs can occupy their thoughts, while people elsewhere are actively engaged in every field of current inquiry and have their eye on all the issues. It is not worth adding anything about the slightly uncivilized manner in which they stare at a foreigner, about the less polite etiquette that permits the most prying looks and uncouth shouts at a foreigner on the street. Where people are so "free" as in America and where minds have so few intellectual preoccupations, there is no reason to marvel if, for example, an American woman in passing laughs right in your face and calls you a "poor Frenchman," or if a black half-ape knocks a dent in your hat with his gold-headed cane. Only the most naive people deplore this, those who have just emigrated from a homeland where people were a little less "free" and etiquette a little more refined.

A native in New Guinea would feel highly insulted if he met an acquaintance on the street and that acquaintance failed to shake his fist at him. This is the friendly form of greeting there. Among certain Malay tribes, two friends meeting after a long separation have to attack each other with abuse, with truly exquisite invective, only to embrace both long and heartily afterward. In America people greet each other with a loud "How do you do?" and hurry by. And before I have time to answer this question, the greeter has gone at least ten steps from me. And so it is that my reply, when it finally comes, lands on the chest of the next fellow I meet—a banana vendor from Sicily or a woman in a bloomer costume. As a greeting, this "How do you do?" is just as meaningless as a friendly clenched fist or a hearty invective; literally translated it means, "By what manner do you do?" This is an imported English greeting, a vulgarized civility from the London suburbs; in English high life one simply never hears it on the street. Only in America is it the height of politeness to come at people with this loud, almost inarticulate "By what manner do you do?" When Americans greet someone, they do so at the top of their lungs.

The greeting is perhaps no more than a relic from less advanced stages of man's development. Why not? It derives undoubtedly from the dog stage. Fine! As long as man has not progressed further than his present stage, the greeting has value as a symbol, as poetry, as respect; it is a manifestation of intelligence that reflects a certain degree of breeding in the nation where it is used—just as it reflects a certain degree of breeding in animals. When the fish became a bird, it learned better manners. The bull greets others quietly and with dignity by staring straight ahead, without saying a word; but cats greet each other on dark nights in such a manner that they really ought to give up the whole idea. But it is *their* greeting—an expression of their temperament and level of development.

The American greeting is a piece of English slang; it is less sensible than audible—a bit of nonsense in words, a shout in passing. Right there on the street a Yankee hurls a meaningless question back at me which I cannot get answered without running after the man. This business of asking me, in front of everyone under the sun, how I "do my do," considering that I left home firmly resolved not to get into a row with anyone, is like waylaying me with an insult at a moment when I am unable to defend myself. The American greeting is so phenomenally absurd that in Norway it would mean *commitment* to use such a greeting.

In America a man walks all the way down a theater aisle with his hat on; he need not be concerned with undue consideration for others. Not until after he has taken his seat and removed his coat, which he then arranges so he can sit on it, not until then does he take off his hat. At vaudeville and comic-opera theaters he does not take his hat off at all; on the other hand, he sheds his coat—in the hot weather, his vest as well. When a Yankee enters the living room of another Yankee, he need not feel at all embarrassed about keeping his hat on; it is the custom in the country to do just as one likes in this regard. If he arrives at mealtime he sits down at the table as one might seat oneself at a workbench, without making any distinction between work and pleasure, without feeling the slightest indebtedness to the host and hostess. It is only at mealtime that a visitor is offered refreshments, and then he takes them for granted as a meal that he might just as well take as leave. He eats like a messenger boy hired to eat, mechanically devouring his beef with great dexterity; he does not *give* himself a treat, he *takes* it, hastily sinking his teeth into the meat and attacking it with a vengeance. The whole thing has to be over in so many minutes; he does not have much time to waste treating anything so inferior as meat with delicacy. And when he is through, he gets up from the table without saying a word, even if he is an invited guest, without so much as a slight nod. His gratitude consists of complete ingratitude. Once I forgot myself and on such an occasion bowed very slightly. My hostess' bewilderment was great, but greater still was mine when she answered: "Thank you, I don't dance!" "No," I replied apologetically, "I also think it is a highly objectionable practice to dance after eating." And we parted.

It is the inanity of American etiquette, its lack of ideality, that makes it national. It is a provincial etiquette from an old, aristocratic land that has been taken over by a nation of brand-new democrats for whom freedom is license and in whom respect is an empty form. When an American lets out a shout as a greeting, a jangle of words in which there is not one particle of sense, then it is a greeting stripped of its ideal, of its evocative content, and is *just* a shout. And when a foreigner, standing at a table, cannot deliver a bow in gratitude for his meal, then this is not unceremoniousness; it is not first and foremost an instance of the "straightforwardness" and "naturalness" for which the Americans have become famous everywhere. On the contrary, it is *empty ceremony*. For, in fact, that is ceremony in America, not expressing one's gratitude for a meal. It is good manners not to. On the other hand, a greeting has to be earsplitting. That too is good manners.

Courtesies are as slight and scant on the streets of America as indoor etiquette is arid and unpleasant.

# Conclusion

*Black Skies*
A nation of patriots hostile to foreigners, a people without a national literature or art, a corrupt society, a materialistic mode of life, and flourishing inanity! Robert Buchanan and Herbert Spencer have dared to make this dangerous statement about America and Americans right in America's midst.

When really free writers in this country have a hero whom they wish well but who has come to grief in his native land because he is a freethinker and a liberal, they send him to America in the last chapter of their book. There is elbowroom there! When our free journalists explain to their subscribers what freedom is, they point to America and say: "There is freedom!" When our extremely advanced women wish to prove how miserably few of their energies they have been allowed to expend in politics and how inferior they are compared to "human beings" elsewhere, then above all they mention America, where women already have become mayors out on some of the prairies. There are women!

You are quickly and easily convinced by America's purely formal development, by the great noise that now attends its name. You hear all the shouting from the election campaigns and are fired up; you listen to the roars from Barnum's circus and tremble; you read the reports from the Chicago hog market and are jubilant; you read every cock-and-bull story in the newspapers, read and believe. After having been deafened by the racket of steam hammers and half-suffocated by steaming machinery, you then think in your befuddled brain: America is big! It is the *big things* that convince you. The American spirit actually slips into your consciousness little by little; you catch it through letters, newspapers, and traveling speakers. The Yankees themselves are completely satisfied with things if they are but large; if they are not large, they must at any rate have cost a great deal of money. It is the scale and cash value of things that constitute their substance. The most elegant palaces on Madison Avenue in Chicago have no more style than a Negro's head; architecturally they are nothing, but they cost a million dollars in cash—which convinces you. The Washington Monument is not in the least interesting except for its height. A shaft stands there 555 feet up in the air. Washington is said to stand on top. It may very well be that he is standing there, but no one sees him. It is impossible to catch sight of the work of art from the ground below. Lake Superior and City Park in Philadelphia are always mentioned in Yankee almanacs as two of America's eleven wonders. Why? Because Lake Superior is the largest lake and City Park is the largest park in the world. The United States has vast prairies; when it is a question of turning a park into a wonder, all it takes is a couple of hundred miles of land, more or less. The Metropolitan Opera House in New York illustrates the Americans' passion for big things. Naturally it is "the largest theater in the world." Its architect went to Europe just for the sake of this theater; he spent a number of weeks in Paris, Vienna, and Moscow, then returned to America and produced a monstrosity of an opera house that is worse than any country's for hearing and seeing. However, it is "the world's largest theater"— which convinces you. A foreigner wants to go; he wants to see the great dramatic art he expects to find there. He is disappointed; he sees cheap entertainment and he does not go there again. Then he goes to Chicago. There he is informed immediately that Madison Square Theater has "the most expensive curtain in the world"; it says so on the placards. "No, no," says the foreigner, shaking his head with determination. "I wanted to see *art*," says he. And resolutely he stands his ground. Time passes; gradually, little by little, the American spirit penetrates his own. He reads the placards, imagines the expensive curtain, hears the electric drum that sounds every evening from six to seven in Madison Square; the publicity takes effect. At last he goes to the theater—in order to see the theater's curtain. The cash value of art has become its substance.

In a similar way, it is easy to be convinced here at home that America is big. Eventually you are overwhelmed by the ballyhoo from there, that fierce and monotonous advertising ballyhoo. When year in and year out you hear nothing about a country except the gigantic things it has, together with their vast scale and enormous cash value, it is not hard ultimately to be overcome with amazement at the mightiness of the nation that has produced them. No one asks about the little things, the *essences* of things; the colossus is the most popular publicity on earth. And one whopper more or less about the American colossi means very little once one has gone so far in one's comprehension that an expanse of land constitutes a park and a curtain dramatic art. America is big!

"America is the country of disillusion and disappointment, in politics, literature, culture, and art; in its scenery, its cities, and its people. With some experience of every country in the civilized world, I can think of none except Russia in which I would not prefer to reside, in which life would not be more worth living, less sordid and mean and unlovely."

America, "the apotheosis of Philistinism, the perplexity and despair of statesmen, the Mecca to which turns every religious or social charlatan, where the only god worshipped is Mammon, and the highest education is the share list; [. . .] where, to enrich jobbers and monopolists and contractors, a nation has emancipated its slaves and enslaved its freemen; where the people is gorged and drunk with materialism [. . .]."

America "boasts of equality and freedom" and "does not understand that [. . .] there is no country where private right and public interests are more systematically outraged than in the United States."*[1]

* Lepel Griffin in 1884: *Fortnightly Review,* I.

Ardent words, dangerous words that mark their man! Perhaps Lepel Griffin will not go to America again under his own name . . . . .

But in all of America is there not an *elite,* a select society of intellectuals, a court of the intellect, a salon, a class, a coterie, cultivated individuals, noble minds?

America is two hundred years old. For one hundred of these years America was completely undeveloped; in the next hundred, good people started coming from Europe—fine people, hardworking thralls, creatures of brawn, bodies whose hands could clear land and whose minds could not think. A generation passed; more and more good people came by square-rigger to Quebec—now and then a bankrupt cafeowner and now and then a pietistical minister followed them. Time passed; a schooner headed into Baltimore with thirty-three thralls on board, five bankrupts, and one manslayer. Time passed; a barque glided into Portmouth's harbor; it held a hundred thralls, a thousand pounds of pastors, a half dozen murderers, fourteen forgers, and twenty thieves. Then one night a merchantman slipped into New Orleans, one night so dark and still, a merchantman so full of wares; it came from the upper Nile and it had seventy blacks in its cargo. They were put ashore; these were creatures of brawn, Negroes from Niam-Niam, whose hands had never cleared land and whose minds had never conceived a thought. And time passed; people came to the land in great, great streams; steam was invented to propel them across the ocean; they flooded Boston, they pushed into New York. Day after day after day great masses of people poured into the prairie kingdom—people of all races and tongues, good people without number: bankrupts and criminals, adventurers and madmen, ministers and Negroes—all members of the pariah race from the entire earth.

And not a noble mind among them.

Among this population, from these individuals America had to establish a cultural elite . . . . .

The country prospered. There was gold in Nevada and California, silver and oil in Pennsylvania, iron, copper, mercury, and lead in Montana, coal in the Allegheny Mountains, in Ohio, Kentucky, and Virginia; there was farming and cattle raising, logging and plantations, fishing and trapping. The sun was hot and the soil rich; fruit ripened on the smallest trees and grass grew on the open road. The good people from every corner of the earth thrived in this new kingdom; they mated and had offspring, enjoyed life, waded in food up to their knees, and ate between three and four times as much as in the old country. And from the thralls came patriots.

From these patriots, among these good people America had to develop its cultural elite . . . . .

How did they go about it? Now there was no culture in the country; good people are not born noble, and when good people later develop into patriots, they become very smug human beings. America's most cultivated minds, the loftiest of them, just those outstanding men who should have been the start of an intellectual elite in the country, placed, out of the smugness of their hearts, a 35 percent duty on the importation of culture—in order to create an elite in their own country. On January 1, 1863, they made the Negroes masters over the Southern freeholders; they took these creatures of brawn from Niam-Niam into their families and gave them their sons and daughters in marriage—in order to beget an elite class of intellectuals!

It is unfair to expect an elite in America; it is more than unreasonable to demand an elite in a country which, when considered as a nation, is purely an experiment and whose people, starting with innate deficiencies, have been fostered in a climate of patriotic hostility to all that is unpatriotic. If one is not born noble in mind and spirit, one must either be ennobled by foreigners or else never be ennobled. Among Americans there is no yearning *beyond* the stars; no more is asked of them than that they be well-born Yankees whose goal is mediocrity, that is, political democracy. In them there is no demanding desire for an aristocracy of the mind, an intellectual sultanate. If there were an aristocratic court of the intellect, why then is it silent in all the realms of the spirit? Where is the class, the coterie, the salon?

But America does have great minds, does it not? Have I perchance gone and forgotten those twenty-one poets included in an encyclopedia, those seven historians, eleven painters, two literary historians, two theologians, one General Grant, one Henry George? I have not gone and forgotten these geniuses. I have not forgotten them on a single page . . . . .

In the fifties there were signs of an intellectual elite in two of the oldest Southern states, but the war came and uprooted it before it was established. Since then it has not shown itself. From that time on, the nation's blood was democratically mixed with that of the Negro, and intelligence sank rather than rose. Cohabitation with the blacks was foisted upon the people. Inhumanity stole them away from Africa where they belong, and democracy transformed them into civilized citizens against the entire order of nature. They have leaped over all the intermediate stages between voracious rat eater and Yankee. Now they are used as preachers, barbers, waiters, and sons-in-law. They have all the rights of a white man and take all the liberties of a black. A Negro is and will remain a Negro. If he shaves a man, he grabs him by the nose as his own blessed grandfather grabbed at a crocodile leg along the Nile; if he serves a meal, he sticks his shiny thumb into the soup all the way up to his elbow. There is no use in rebuking him for his slightly uncivilized manner of doing things. If you are not rudely answered back, the African democrat will at least tell you in an insulted voice to "mind your own business!" And then you have to hold your tongue; the discussion is at an end. Still, if you are right, and you are sitting there with two big fists, then you swallow your food with little appetite. Of course, it would be another matter if you had expressly ordered soup with thumbs.

The Negroes are and will remain Negroes, an nascent human form from the tropics, creatures with entrails in their heads, rudimentary organs on the body of a white society.

Instead of founding an intellectual elite, America has established a mulatto studfarm; therefore one might be justified in seeking an intellectual elite in countries where there are greater chances for its existence than in America. It does not necessarily follow, because there is an elite in every established land with a long history and a richly varied contemporary culture, that there is also an elite in a newly discovered land with no national history and an old, effete culture. One cannot reasonably demand more of an intellectual elite in America than what the clergy has fashioned in four generations. What there is, is situated in Boston. It operates quietly; it shatters no worlds and shakes no earths.

If, then, it is unreasonable to demand culture of the Americans because their temperament and social organization largely preclude it, it is surely excusable in part that they have no culture. However, you do not risk life and limb by quietly mentioning this; it is safest to remain completely silent. The inexperienced person who makes excuses for America's cultural barrenness in the presence of an American will be asked on the spot to come and make something of it—just come on! So the Americans are not completely blameless when they reject all foreign guidance purely because of their thin-skinned egotism; one has to search far into the past to find a nation that has kept its cultural life that barren simply because of jealous national vanity. There is reason to doubt progress that comes gradually, step by step—the small improvements and minor special reforms that are fought for today only to be totally obliterated by the next generation; so instead one can only put one's faith in the great chess moves, the mighty revolts of individual geniuses who suddenly thrust mankind forward for several generations. But what then if the time is not ripening for a historical revolt, if the ground is not being prepared for the shoots of intellectual possibility in a country? If, on the contrary, the land is being put by, fenced in, left standing with wild vegetation and weeds in profusion? An overgrown national park, a vast wonder of a park! It is every American's primary mission in life to be a patriotic citizen of the great prairies rather than to become a mature individual within the entire human race. This feeling has penetrated and colored all their notions from the cradle on; only by being an American is one truly a human being. Therefore, not one doubter can be found in that whole wide country—a seeker of the light, a rebellious spirit who could kick over the traces, fall out of step, take the first deliberate misstep to the miserable and foolish pipings of the penny whistles. Everyone goes merrily along amid loud hurrahs, without ever looking around . . . . .

A world of shouting and steam and great groaning stamping machines; a kingdom of that world with people from every zone, from the whites of the north to the apes and intellectual mulattoes of the tropics; a land with light, fertile topsoil and a preserve of primordial spaces.

And black skies . . . . .

# Editor's Notes

The preparation of this text, both the translation and annotation, has raised a number of problems in regard to sources and editing procedures. After three quarters of a century, some of Hamsun's references, for example, have simply proven too ephemeral, too vague, or too inaccurate for verification; in other instances it is impossible to ascertain whether he worked with primary or secondary sources. Two sources require special mention. The selections from Whitman's poetry, which is frequently cited in Hamsun's discussion of the poet, reflect the seventh edition of *Leaves of Grass*—the 1881–82 edition that established the final arrangement, titles, and textual revisions of the poems—but Hamsun's exact text is unknown. There is some evidence, however, that he used a popular abridgment issued in the Canterbury Poets series, *Leaves of Grass: The Poems of Walt Whitman (Selected)*, introduction by Ernest Rhys (London, 1886). Among other factors, he refers to Rhys by name; his citations are limited to the poems contained in the abridgment; and in one instance he reverses the order of two poems in the "Calamus" group, "Full of Life Now" and "That Shadow My Likeness," which is one of the idiosyncrasies of the Canterbury Poets edition. In my notes, the poems are identified only by title and, where relevant, section, since editions are widely available; but their textual accuracy has been checked against Whitman's *Leaves of Grass,* Inclusive Edition, edited by Emory Holloway (Garden City, N.Y., 1926). Hamsun's edition of *Representative Men* is similarly unidentifiable. All references in the notes are to Volume IV, the Centenary edition of *The Complete Works of Ralph Waldo Emerson,* 12 vols. (Boston: Houghton, Mifflin and Co., 1903–1904), hereafter cited as *Works.* Because the Emerson quotations, in contrast to most of the poetry excerpts, are so tightly worked into the fabric of Hamsun's analysis and evaluation, the page references and often the original passages are supplied in the notes for ready comparison.

Although the translation conforms closely to both content and format of the original, certain tacit emendations have been made in the spelling of English words or names and in minor details of punctuation and quotation. Moreover, in regard to quoted material in the text, bracketed ellipses to signal undisclosed omissions have been introduced in those instances where the original is not cited in the notes; otherwise omissions are evident by collation. All known sources are identified, but lesser discrepancies in the quoted material, such as alterations in tense, minor translational variations, as well as Hamsun's occasional insertion of exclamation points, question marks, and italics, are not specifically noted. Although this procedure may conceal multiple deviations from the original, it has the merit of not overburdening the annotative apparatus with minutiae.

The reader should bear in mind, however, that some misquotation, whether intentional or unintentional, occurs in many of Hamsun's prose and verse renderings, and this is preserved in the text. Such inaccuracy is explained in part by Hamsun's statement to Victor Nilsson at the time of publication: he had no reference books available, just his "memory and a number of notations scattered about in lectures and notebooks." Too rigorous attention to the niceties of twentieth-century documentation would thus seem to distort the spirit and intention of the book; for despite the facade of scholarly appurtenances, it is in essence an intensely personal document, often literary rather than factual in its inspiration and moulded throughout by an individual temperament and point of view. This does not mean, of course, that Hamsun's use of source materials for documentation and support has not been carefully examined for accuracy of content, reliability, and completeness. Where significant discrepancies do appear, the original text is cited in the notes and, when necessary, discussed. Inevitably in such an evaluative process, a border area exists between minor or accidental error and possible misrepresentation, between translational variation and misreading, and the judgment of the editor then becomes particularly visible and vulnerable.

## THE CULTURAL CLIMATE

1. Since President Taylor, who died in 1850, never traveled abroad, the writer is probably Bayard Taylor, American journalist, traveler, and author, who in 1857 published a description of Sweden, Lapland, and Norway entitled *Northern Travel*.

2. In contrast to Hamsun's earlier reproduction of the "Balance Sheet of the World, 1870–1880," cited only by page and author's name, and the material from an unnamed work on U.S. agriculture attributed to Edward Atkinson, this quotation provides the first documentation that can be

collated with its source, the December 20, 1888, issue of *America*. Although Hamsun volunteers no information about this obscure political and literary weekly, edited in Chicago by Slason Thompson and Hobart C. Taylor, the December issue is the primary source of confirmation for the views in his study; in fact, his citations are confined to the "Americanisms" column in this one issue which had come into his hands because it contains his article on August Strindberg.

The political orientation of *America*, described as "a journal for Americans," had its origin in the Know-Nothing movement of the 1850s. In the course of publication from April 1888 to September 1891, when it merged with the *Graphic*, it backed the American Party of 1888 because, as Thompson editorialized in a July 14, 1888, article on "American Principles," the Democratic and Republican parties had failed to deal with "the great and pressing questions that confront and imperil republican institutions to-day—indiscriminate immigration, unrestricted facility of naturalization, ignorance at the polls, and servility to alienism in elections." Among his recommendations for reform were "the restriction and Americanizing of immigration, and the protection of our people from the vitiating stream of humanity drawn hither from the lowest levels of European misery, disease and crime." This proposal, as he had indicated a week earlier in "Protection against Imported Labor," was specifically directed at the importation of pauper labor, particularly Italians, who he felt were glutting the American labor market and depressing the wages of American workingmen.

It was thus in keeping with the journal's editorial bias that its regular, unsigned column "Americanisms" contained a brief notice concerning the Immigration Committee in Congress: "The State Department has received nearly a hundred replies from consuls in Europe to the questions sent out by Chairman Ford, of the Immigration Committee. They show that in nearly all large foreign cities a regularly organized business is carried on of shipping emigrants to this country. The character of the people with whom the United States is being flooded is fully set forth. The reports bear out fully every charge made by *America* before the committee's investigation was begun. It will be interesting to note the reply of H. Albert Johnson, Consul at Venice, Italy, who says: 'Emigrants are recruited from those people whom, as a rule, their native country does not wish to retain. They are often fugitives from justice, and, in many cases, those leaving their native countries to evade legitimate duties imposed by law—men whose stupendous ignorance is unequaled by any other class of people found in the civilized world. They are no more fitted to perform the duties of citizenship than slaves newly released from bondage. They have no intention of becoming citizens of the United

States. They desire simply to get more money for their work, and to decrease as much as possible the amount of work to be done for the money received.' These words should be firmly impressed upon the mind of every patriotic American citizen, and remembered as the truth concerning the greatest evil of the present day" (p. 5).

Comparison establishes a number of significant discrepancies involving both suppression and distortion on Hamsun's part. As is evident, the item supports the weekly's position on the importation of pauper labor, whereas Hamsun introduces the material to substantiate his contention that Americans, because of their "celestial self-sufficiency," are unwilling to acknowledge the need for foreign labor; misguided nationalism is thus the sole cause for the proposals to restrict immigration. Nor does the *America* account mention any solicitation of patriotic support from American consuls (whom Hamsun elevates to ministerial rank). The Immigration Committee's questionnaire appears confined to questions about foreign recruiting practices and the character of the recruits, and this is also the relevance of the comments from the Venetian consul, whose name is suppressed. It will be noted, too, that what Hamsun summarizes as a pathetic description of Italian immigrants—"their poverty, their rags"—in Johnson's reply is actually a general assessment of the moral and intellectual caliber of emigrants recruited from foreign countries—an assessment that wins Hamsun's wholehearted endorsement elsewhere in his study. The remainder of the Johnson quotation is therefore not only inaccurately limited to Italians; it is cited out of context. Its calculated effect on Scandinavian audiences is obvious.

3. In June 1865, Secretary James Harlan discharged Whitman from a clerkship in the Department of the Interior, but in July he was rehired by the Attorney General's office. This misdating, which is repeated in the Whitman section, may come from an error in the Rhys introduction to *Leaves of Grass*. In commenting on Whitman's dismissal and William Douglas O'Connor's subsequent defense of Whitman against charges of obscenity in his poetry, Rhys notes: "This was in 1868" (p. xxii). Actually O'Conner's pamphlet, *The Good Gray Poet: A Vindication,* was published in New York in 1866.

4. Although Hamsun cites "inter alia" the January 1879 issue of the *International Review* for confirmation of his literary sketch, his source was presumably an unsigned critique under the heading "Contemporary Literature," which appeared in the November issue—the sole reference to Welles in the journal for that year. Whether or not Hamsun had also read *Bohême* is of course impossible to ascertain; his critical estimate of the man is in any event his own. A comparison of his presentation and the reference exposes, nevertheless, a number of discrepancies: "When

one says that Mr. Welles's 'Bohême' is as poor a collection of more or less perfectly rhymed lines as one often sees, one does the book justice. The author has evidently read, possibly in a desultory way, Shelley, Browning, Swinburne, and our own F. S. Saltus, the American Baudelaire; but the reading of his poems cannot be conscientiously recommended to any one. To tear the book to pieces would be an odious task; there is no harm in the poetry, and possibly in the future Mr. Welles will have more to say to the world than he has yet said. In that case, his evidently early practice will probably do him good. Meanwhile, it is with perfect sincerity and no intention of wounding him, that we advise him to wait before publishing until he is forced to write, rather than to rush again into print without any message to deliver. A repetition of this offence will call for capital punishment. The first time is but a venial sin, an intended compliment to letters" (p. 572). Thus the criticism is obviously irrelevant to the charge of literary suppression: it does not turn on the invidious effects of foreign influence upon artistic merit; it simply notes the lack of significant artistic content in an otherwise innocuous, apparently youthful collection of poems. Nor is the account of the poet's literary contacts accurately represented since, rather than de Musset, Welles appears to have read an American counterpart of Baudelaire, Francis Saltus Saltus. All in all, despite the fact that he never became well known in American letters, Welles's fate scarcely seems attributable to the almost paternal admonishments of this reviewer.

5. The source of this quotation from the ninth edition of the *Encyclopaedia Britannica* is a seventeen-page article by the English scholar John Nichol, entitled "American Literature," in which he discusses the dependence of American writers upon English literary and intellectual traditions, noting specifically: "If the people of the United States had spoken a language of their own, it is probable they would have gained in originality; as it is, they are only now beginning to sign their intellectual declaration of independence—a fact confessed among the latest words of their own greatest prose artist:—'Bred in English habits of thought as most of us are, we have not yet modified our instincts to the necessities of our new modes of life. Our philosophers have not yet taught us what is best, nor have our poets sung to us what is most beautiful in the kind of life that we must lead, and therefore we still read the old English wisdom, and harp upon the ancient strings.'" Although unidentified here, the author quoted is apparently Nathaniel Hawthorne, who is subsequently described as "on the whole the most artistic of American prose writers" (p. 726).

6. In again raising the charge of ascendent materialism first voiced in his articles of 1885, Hamsun introduces here the ostensibly authoritative

testimony of Robert Buchanan, whose "Free Thought in America" actually appeared in the April 1885 issue of the *North American Review*, CXL, 316–327. His quotation, which is both truncated and somewhat altered from the original, is part of Buchanan's caustic disparagement of Robert Ingersoll in his cause against orthodox religious belief: "The predominant vices of America, especially as represented by its great cities, are its irreverence, its recklessness, its impatience—in one word, its materialism. A nation in which the artistic sense is almost dead, which is practically without a literature, which is impatient of all sanctions and indifferent to all religions, which is corrupt from the highest pinnacle of its public life down to the lowest depth of its primalism, which is at once thin-skin'd under criticism and aggressive to criticise, which worships material forces in every shape and form, which despises conventional conditions, yet is slavish to ignoble fashions, which, too hasty to think for itself, takes recklessly at second-hand any old- or new-clothes philosophy that may be imported from Europe, yet, while wearing the raiment openly, mocks and ridicules the civilization that wove the fabric—such a nation, I think, might be spared the spectacle of an elderly gentleman in modern costume trampling on the lotus, the rose, and the lily in the gardens of the gods" (pp. 316–317). According to Hamsun, this telling characterization of Buchanan's countrymen, written with a "heavy heart," its authority reinforced by the venerable age and religious orthodoxy of the author, had evoked prolonged censure and abuse. But an examination of the authorship, tone, and content of the article, as well as subsequent reader response, refutes this account. The poet, dramatist, and frequent periodical contributor, Robert Williams Buchanan (1841–1901), was not American but British; and his article, obviously written in his mid-forties, was chiefly concerned with his largely sympathetic views on O. E. Frothingham and reflected, after his eloquent dismissal of American culture and moral values, an intense interest in questions concerning free thought or "radical religion." If, as Hamsun implies, he had indeed followed reader reaction to the article (two letters to the editor under "Comments" in the May and June issues), he would have discovered both that Buchanan was "an English critic" and "distinguished Briton" and that one commentator also joined in deploring the materialism of the age and acknowledged the need for "a more humanizing humanity."

## LITERATURE

1. Although the text assigns Talmage's views on the Sunday newspapers to a lecture on the subject, Hamsun's source of information is again a brief item in the "Americanisms" column of *America* for December 20, 1888—an item that also contains the editorial comment that he

subsequently represents as a separate "five-line article": "The Rev. T. De Witt Talmage recently made the following statement concerning Sunday newspapers: 'They have come to stay, and reformists in and out of newspaperdom should direct their efforts toward making them better, raising their standard of morality, and causing them to become a medium of accomplishing great good. The newspapers have more than kept pace with the world. Compare the average journal of to-day with what was published thirty-five years ago, and you would be surprised to see the step upward in the publication of better literature. The men employed upon newspapers to-day are better than they were thirty-five years ago. Their productions are more healthy, and thus the tone of the secular press is improving rapidly from a religious and moral point of view. Morality in the newspaper is as good as morality in the pulpit. Yes, the Sunday paper has come to stay.' If the average Sunday journal of to-day were compared to the paper of thirty-five years ago we would find that the latter was moral in its tone and patriotic in its utterances, while the former is a hodgepodge of sensation, scurrility, and scandal, with a flavoring of seriousness. The morality of the Sunday newspaper may be the equal of that of the pulpit, but this is a woful confession for a divine to make" (p. 6). It will be noted that there are two alterations in Hamsun's translation which serve to broaden the context of the quotation and to heighten the contrast between the Sunday and the daily papers. Talmage's statement specifically concerns the "Sunday newspapers," which he considers a permanent feature of American journalism, but Hamsun relates his remarks to "the American press in general," which has grown settled. The *America* rebuttal, on the other hand, contrasts "the average Sunday journal of to-day" with "the paper of thirty-five years ago"—a comparison that Hamsun represents as "our *Sunday papers* of to-day" and "the average *daily paper* of thirty-five years ago." Granting that the wording of the former comparison is possibly ambiguous, the general context nevertheless indicates that the *America* statement is limited to the Sunday papers; in no event does it support the emphatic translation of "average *daily paper*."

2. Whatever Hamsun's source, it is not the *Boston Globe* for this date.

3. Despite errors in the initial place and date of publication for *Leaves of Grass* (actually Brooklyn, 1855), the origin of the information in these paragraphs seems to be either an article by the Danish critic Rudolf Schmidt, "Walt Whitman, det amerikanske Demokratis Digter," in *For Idé og Virkelighed*, I (1872), 152–216, or Kristofer Janson's study of American conditions, *Amerikanske Forholde, Fem Foredrag* (Copenhagen, 1881), which not only presents a critical discussion of Whitman but also incorporates extensive material from the Schmidt essay. As a

result, both sources contain an excerpt from an unsigned article (by Edward Dowden) in the *Westminster Review*, XCVI (July 1872), 33–68, entitled "The Poetry of Democracy: Walt Whitman," which provides Hamsun with the phrase "fact of world dimensions." Although Hamsun incorrectly ascribes the statement to Whitman and Schmidt, the discrepancy between the English "fact of the universe" and the text formulation is necessitated by his humorous manipulation of the Danish word *Verdenskendsgjærning* and the progression "cosmos, outer space, or the universe": "At last steps forward a man unlike any of his predecessors, and announces himself, and is announced with a flourish of critical trumpets, as Bard of America, and Bard of democracy. What cannot be questioned after an hour's acquaintance with Walt Whitman and his 'Leaves of Grass,' is that in him we meet a man not shaped out of old-world clay, not cast in any old-world mould, and hard to name by any old-world name. In his self-assertion there is a manner of powerful nonchalantness which is not assumed; he does not peep timidly from behind his works to glean our sufferages, but seems to say, 'Take me or leave me, here I am, a solid and not inconsiderable fact of the universe'" (p. 36).

4. "From Paumanok Starting I Fly Like a Bird." Here in the literary section of his book, as elsewhere, Hamsun has translated all of the verse and prose passages, with the exception of Whitman's "Still Though the One I Sing" and an occasional English gloss. His translations are therefore rerendered in English and retain his alterations throughout, but only significant deviations are identified in the notes, either by quoting the original text for comparison (as in note 5 below) or by other comment.

5. "Starting from Paumanok," sec. 16:

> The red aborigines,
> Leaving natural breaths, sounds of rain and winds, calls as of
>    birds and animals in the woods, syllabled to us for names,
> Okonee . . . Walla-Walla,
> Leaving such to the States they melt, they depart, charging the
>    water and the land with names.

6. "Still Though the One I Sing."

7. As specific details in his ensuing Whitman portrait clearly indicate, Hamsun was either familiar with O'Connor's *The Good Gray Poet* or at least O'Connor's description of the poet which Rhys cites in his introduction to *Leaves of Grass*, pp. xii–xiii (see the introductory comments to my notes). Richard Maurice Bucke, who wrote the first complete biography, *Walt Whitman* (Philadelphia, 1883), is also mentioned in the

latter source. Similarly, Hamsun's knowledge of Moncure D. Conway may have come directly from his article, "Walt Whitman," *Fortnightly Review*, VI (October 15, 1866), 538–548, or from secondary references in both Janson's book and Schmidt's essay.

8. "Starting from Paumanok," sec. 3.

9. *Ibid.*, sec. 4:

> I conn'd old times,
> I sat studying at the feet of the great masters,
> Now if eligible O that the great masters might return and
> study me.

10. Sec. 2.

11. There are, *inter alia*, numerous translational errors in the catalogue.

12. Deriving ultimately from the preface to *The Marble Fawn*, the immediate source of this quotation is probably Nichol's *Encyclopedia Britannica* article "American Literature," which would account for its elliptical form though not the alterations in meaning. In the article the quotation, actually two successive quotes, is introduced to explain Hawthorne's having chosen an Italian setting for his novel: "There is in our country no shadow, no ambiguity, no mystery, no picturesque and gloomy wrong." "Romance and poetry, ivy, lichens, and wallflowers, need ruin to make them grow" (p. 727).

13. Sec. 1.

14. "Shut Not Your Doors."

15. "For You O Democracy."

16. "Full of Life Now."

17. "That Shadow My Likeness."

18. Secs. 4, 5. In addition to an omission at the beginning of the first quote, its conclusion should read: "I think whoever I see must be happy."

19. The source of this judgment is unknown. It contradicts, however, Nichol's statement in "American Literature" that, although Emerson was probably most widely known in Britain for this book, it was "by no means the most satisfactory of his works" (p. 730).

20. *Works*, p. 78. In identifying Hamsun's quotations from *Representative Men*, multiple page references for a given paragraph in the text are listed sequentially in a single note. A colon following a page reference indicates that the ensuing quotation or comment relates to that reference (see note 22 below).

21. Quote unknown.

22. *Works*, pp. 12; 40; 39–40. Pages 42–43: The quotation from the

*Republic,* together with the allusions to Solon, Sophron, and Socrates, belongs to Emerson's own examination of the range of Plato's intellectual background that entitled him to the status of "representative of philosophy." In this context Emerson quotes Plato as saying: "Such a genius as philosophers must of necessity have, is wont but seldom in all its parts to meet in one man, but its different parts generally spring up in different persons."

23. Henry Norman, "Ralph Waldo Emerson: An Ethical Study," *Fortnightly Review,* n.s. XXXIV (1883), 423.

24. *Works,* p. 27.

25. *Ibid.,* p. 284. The misreadings in this passage and their perpetuation in Hamsun's ensuing argument become apparent by comparing it with the original. Note, also, the suppression of the later portion of the final sentence which relates "culture" not to general progress, as Hamsun indicates, but to Goethe's own intellectual development: "He has not worshipped the highest unity; he is incapable of a self-surrender to the moral sentiment. There are nobler strains in poetry than any he has sounded . . . His is not even the devotion to pure truth; but to truth for the sake of culture. He has no aims less large than the conquest of universal nature, of universal truth, to be his portion: a man not to be bribed, nor deceived, nor overawed; of a stoical self-command and self-denial, and having one test for all men—*What can you teach me?*"

26: *Ibid.,* pp. 210; 204; 208; 211; 214; 212; 204. Page 195: In discussing Shakespeare's literary indebtedness, Emerson cites Malone's finding in regard to *Henry VI,* Parts I–III, that "out of 6043 lines, 1771 were written by some author preceding Shakespeare, 2373 by him, on the foundation laid by his predecessors, and 1899 were entirely his own." Emerson then adds, "And the proceeding investigation hardly leaves a single drama of his absolute invention." 198. Page 199: "It is easy to see that what is best written or done by genius in the world, was no man's work, but came by wide social labor, when a thousand wrought like one, sharing the same impulse." 198; 199–200.

27. Against the background of Emerson's genteel, ministerial heritage, Hamsun here puts his finger on the fundamental conflict between literary criteria and moral requirements in Emerson's ultimate assessment of Shakespeare the poet; however, whether for satiric effect or from a misunderstanding of language—or both—he introduces a number of inaccuracies into the criticism assigned to Emerson. Throughout Hamsun's analysis, for example, Shakespeare's private life and personal conduct are variously represented as "frivolous," "sinful," "disreputable," "low," "unholy," and "lusty." But as the Shakespeare essay makes clear, it is Emerson's puritanical distrust of the theater that leads him to dis-

parage Shakespeare's employment as actor and purveyor of public amusement, and then not because of any imputed personal immorality in connection with these activities, but simply because of their worldly and trifling nature. They lack moral seriousness. The assertion that Shakespeare was guilty of excesses in his behavior may thus be a fillip added by Hamsun to heighten the defects in Emerson's reasoning and critical insights. There is also evidence that he misread the original text, for his interpretation appears to come from an undercurrent of innuendo detected in his quotation from *Works*, p. 218, beginning: "The Egyptian verdict of the Shakespeare Societies comes to mind; that he was a jovial actor and manager." Unaccountably, Hamsun renders this as "The Shakespeare Society has brought to light that Shakespeare took part in and provided lively entertainment (*Lystigheder*)"—a translation that may be contaminated by Emerson's earlier statement that Shakespeare was "master of the revels to mankind" (p. 217). In any event, the comment simply reiterates facts about Shakespeare's life garnered by the Shakespeare Societies: "He was a good-natured sort of man, an actor and shareholder in the theatre, not in any striking manner distinguished from other actors and managers" (p. 205). What is curious about Hamsun's rendering is, first, that in his subsequent use of the adjective *lystig*, he specifically identifies it as the Norwegian gloss for Emerson's "jovial" and, second, that *lystig* (merry, wanton, lusty) does not really correspond to Emerson's word. A further misapprehension occurs in connection with Emerson's next line: "I cannot marry this fact to his verse." Hamsun's judgmental rendering is: "I can find no pleasure in this demeaning fact." The subsequent clause, "we might leave the fact in the twilight of fate," is also incorrectly expanded to "we could surrender his life." It is the conclusion of the passage, however, that seems to provide substance for Hamsun's assertion of loose behavior, turning on Emerson's statement that "it must even go into the world's history that the best poet led an obscure and profane life, using his genius for the public amusement." As will be noted, Hamsun inaccurately translates "obscure" as "low," and "profane" as "unholy," although in this context the meaning of the latter is "nonreligious" or "secular" and points up Emerson's profound disappointment that Shakespeare failed to unite the roles of poet and priest. In pursuing this misinterpretation with its mounting, humorous orchestration of apparent contradictions in this and previous passages, Hamsun again mentions the excesses in Shakespeare's frivolous existence; at the same time he faults Emerson for being displeased with the finding that Shakespeare was "lusty" (*lystig*), Emerson's "jovial." Now, however, Hamsun plays this characteristic off against the Societies' seemingly contradictory discovery that Shakespeare "in all respects appears as a good husband, with no reputation for eccentricity or excess" (p. 205). The innuendo in the query—"wherein was he then lusty?"—lodges in Hamsun's emphatic rendering of the first phrase, coupled with his suppression of the amplifying material.

28. *Works*, p. 15.

29. *Ibid.*, pp. 70–74. Although this lengthy quotation contains several translational errors—for example, Emerson's comment that Socrates "knew the old characters" and "valued the bores and philistines" is rendered as "knew the old titles" and "knew how to distinguish between bores and philistines"—they are largely insignificant.

30. The epithet "ignorant intellect," which does not occur in Emerson's text, may be Hamsun's distillation of the original description: "A pitiless disputant, who knows nothing, but the bounds of whose conquering intelligence no man had ever reached; whose temper was imperturbable; whose dreadful logic was always leisurely and sportive; so careless and ignorant as to disarm the wariest and draw them, in the pleasantest manner into horrible doubts and confusion" (*ibid.*, p. 73).

31. *Ibid.*, pp. 223; 225–226; 227; 228–229; 233.

32. *Ibid.*, pp. 253–256.

33. *Ibid.*, p. 258.

34. The reference is to Henry Norman's essay, identified above.

35. Cited by Norman, p. 431.

36. *Works*, pp. 47–48. Including the material in Hamsun's ellipsis, the final portion of this series should read: "The mind is urged to ask for one cause of many effects; then for the cause of that; and again the cause, diving still into the profound: self-assured that it shall arrive at an absolute and sufficient one—a one that shall be all. 'In the midst of the sun is the light, in the midst of the light is truth, and in the midst of truth is the imperishable being,' say the Vedas." Hamsun's use of the formula "a fundamental unity," rather than "a one that shall be all," appears to derive from Emerson's subsequent statement that "in all nations there are minds which incline to dwell in the conception of the fundamental Unity" (p. 49).

37. What is here presented as the sole tendency of these cardinal "elements" is the final tendency of the dual philosophic principles of the ideal and real in a development that begins: "If speculation tends thus to a terrific unity, in which all things are absorbed, action tends directly backwards to diversity. The first is the course or gravitation of mind; the second is the power of nature. Nature is the manifold. The unity absorbs, and melts or reduces. Nature opens and creates. These two principles reappear and interpenetrate all things, all thought; the one, the many . . . and, if we dare carry these generalizations a step higher, and name

the last tendency of both, we might say, that the end of the one is escape from organization,—pure science; and the end of the other is the highest instrumentality, or use of means, or executive deity" (*ibid.*, pp. 51–52).

38. *Ibid.*, p. 52.

39. *Ibid.*, pp. 40; 29. Pages 81–82: "He represents the privilege of the intellect, the power, namely, of carrying up every fact to successive platforms and so disclosing in every fact a germ of expansion . . . These expansions or extensions consist in continuing the spiritual sight where the horizon falls on our natural vision, and by this second sight discovering the long lines of law which shoot in every direction. Everywhere he stands on a path which has no end, but runs continuously round the universe." Page 83: The reference is not to the immortality of the soul but Plato's perception of "the laws of return, or reaction, which secure instant justice throughout the universe." The source of the first half of the quotation about the nature of man's soul is obscure; the second is slightly misquoted (p. 70). 58, see below; 44. Page 58: Emerson is discussing Plato's theory of divine inspiration: "He believes that poetry, prophecy and the high insight are from a wisdom of which man is not master; that the gods never philosophize, but by a celestial mania these miracles are accomplished. Horsed on these winged steeds, he sweeps the dim regions, visits worlds which flesh cannot enter." Page 45: "Here are all its traits, already discernible in the mind of Plato,—and in none before him. It has spread itself since into a hundred histories, but has added no new element . . . How Plato came thus to be Europe, and philosophy, and almost literature, is the problem for us to solve." Page 78: "The acutest German, the lovingest disciple, could never tell what Platonism was; indeed, admirable texts can be quoted on both sides of every great question from him."

40. *Ibid.*, p. 189.

41. *Ibid.*, p. 42.

42. This may be a mistranslation of "the keen street and market debater" (*ibid.*, p. 75); see also note 30 above.

43. Despite obvious disparities in tone and treatment, this development is indebted to the Norman essay and its elucidation of Emerson's belief in an intuitive apprehension of God as a function of the basic, if seemingly contradictory, aspects of his intellectual makeup—the one, mystical, with its roots in Platonic idealism; the other, "Yankee," which sprang unconsciously from the realism of his New England, Puritan background. "So far as Emerson commits himself to any definite view," Norman writes in regard to the former, "he does so to a belief in the existence of one all-embracing, all-creating mind, to which the finite mind can have access, and thus obtain knowledge of absolute truth. The

inviolate soul is in perpetual telegraphic communication with the source of events.' In one of his less-known writings (Introduction to Goodwin's translation of Plutarch's *Morals*) he puts the same thought very strongly and far less figuratively: 'The central fact is the superhuman intelligence pouring into us from its unknown fountain, to be received with religious awe, and defended from any mixture with our will'" (p. 424). And he adds later: "He believes that knowledge comes directly from the infinite to the finite mind; that when the 'inviolate soul' is in need of information it receives it in the shape of a telegraphic message from the 'source of events;' that truth is with ourselves and will issue in its native purity if we but strip off the coverings in which the experience of our life and the experience of our will have enveloped it; that 'undoubtedly we have no questions to ask which are unanswerable;' that ignorance exists only in connection with impurity of heart; in short, that instead of searching for truth, the wise man listens for it" (p. 428). *Works*, p. 186: The quotation adduced as proof of the soul's immortality concludes the Montaigne essay and relates to Emerson's certitude of an all-embracing, beneficent "Eternal Cause." He cites the line from W. E. Channing's "A Poet's Hope." Pages 182–183: The concluding "and death" is not in the original text.

44. *Works*, p. 174. "Knowledge is the knowing that we can not know." The quote on "details," one of several "oracular utterances" illustrating the priority of mind over matter in Emerson's view, is cited by Norman (p. 424).

## THE VISUAL ARTS

1. The source Hamsun cites in his footnote is inaccurately identified and unknown.

2. This line echoes Lepel Griffin's observation in "A Visit to Philistia," *Fortnightly Review*, n.s. XXV (January 1884), 50–64, from which Hamsun later takes a number of quotations: "Annually, a flight of pork-packers and successful tradesmen cross the Atlantic, with their families, to complete an education, which has in reality never begun, by a contemplation of Paris hotels and Rhine steamboats" (p. 55).

3. The reference apparently invokes an article by the English art critic Philip Gilbert Hamerton, "English and American Painting at Paris in 1878, I," *International Review*, VI (1879), 113–132. Here, in appraising American contributions to the French Universal Exhibition of 1878, Hamerton commented—although scarcely in a statement of official American policy—that the American works lacked artistic nationality. He attributed this to the fact that American art students in Paris had so thoroughly acquired the processes and spirit of French art

that it would be impossible to distinguish between the productions of the two nationalities if all were exhibited under French names. This influence was not necessarily detrimental, however: "I am not sure that in the interests of the future American school this can be considered a great misfortune, though it is destructive of originality for the present. Every nation in which a new school is formed must learn to paint from some other nation which has already mastered the art. England learned the art from Flanders, America is learning it from France. *Is learning it,* do I say? nay, rather, has already learned it, for Parisian Americans seem to paint just as well as the French themselves, and I think the time has come for the development of a more national style on your side of the Atlantic. It was well at the beginning, when you knew nothing, to go to those who did know, and get taught; but now that you know as much as your masters (I mean of all communicable knowledge) why not quietly go home and work out your own artistic destinies in your own way?" (p. 114).

## DRAMATIC ART

1. For sheer humbug, Hamsun's ostensibly authoritative comment on Kean, Booth, and Murphey is unrivaled elsewhere in his book. It is uncertain, for example, whether Hamsun's "refined, appealing, long-haired," gentlemanly Kean is the English tragedian Edmund Kean (1787–1833); his less illustrious son Charles (1811–1868), whose reputation rested primarily on his lavish Shakespeare revivals rather than on his acting; or even Thomas Kean, who together with Walter Murray briefly toured the eastern seaboard in the mid-eighteenth century. In any event, despite the audaciously convincing bluff of actual encounter, theater history records no Kean of American birth and stage education, distinguished for his thoroughly original reading of Hamlet. The unidentifiable Murphey, too, remains a unique Hamsun experience, although he may have had in mind the Irish-born tragedian John McCullough, who died in 1885. Hamsun's Edwin Booth, on the other hand, is accurately identified as the brother of Lincoln's assassin, and he did belong to a family of actors famous in American theater history. By 1889 he was approaching the end of his career because of failing health, but earlier, before April 1865, he had won immense popularity with American audiences; his one hundred performances of Hamlet in 1864 established a record unsurpassed until John Barrymore's one hundred and one consecutive performances in 1923.

Although Hamsun's biographies are therefore unreliable and in part fictive, there is some evidence that he confounded his sources and that his Kean, if Edmund, is in part Booth and vice versa. Booth was widely acclaimed for his roles in Shakespearean tragedy and, deeply affected by the insanity of his father, brother, and second wife, was himself subject to periods of severe depression. In contrast, Kean was notorious for his scandalous living. Contemporary accounts pronounced him temperamentally incapable of the qualities required for Romeo or Hamlet, but the malevolence of his Shylock at Drury Lane in 1814 brought him immediate success, and Richard the Second and Iago have been judged among his best roles (see Phyllis Hartnoll, ed., *The Oxford Companion to the Theatre* (London, 1951)).

2. Edvard Brandes, who was himself an experienced theater critic in Denmark, confessed that he was unfamiliar with a "sliding scene" and questioned whether Hamsun was referring to nothing more unusual than a movable backdrop. See his newspaper review of Hamsun's book, "Literatur," *Politiken*, April 28, 1889.

3. Although the flattering allusion to Kean's artistic highmindedness does not inspire confidence, Hamsun's reference to the involvement of four well-known theater personalities—Edwin Booth, Joseph Jefferson, Lawrence Barrett, and Dion Boucicault—suggests that he possessed more information than is now accessible in the December 20, 1888, issue of *America*. This source does not account for Hamsun's entire presentation, but it does contain the second Boucicault quotation and the brief *America* comment, both of which have been somewhat altered: "The American 'mummers' are now demanding protection against the influx of pauper-paid actors from Europe. They are quite right in their demands, but it is questionable as to whether English actors can be considered paupers. Considering the financial success of the English stars who appear in the American firmament, it would seem that the Americans come more nearly under the title of paupers. The English, however, are contract laborers, and as such should be excluded. Speaking of this, Mr. Dion Boucicault recently said: 'I don't see why, if the trades and industries of this country are to be protected in regard to imported labor, our profession should be exempt. I think the movement an excellent one, and I hope it will go through. The pushing to the front seats in Thespian circles of English and other European actors and actresses is simply a piece of cadism on the part of the American public. The American actors and actresses are by far the best in the world, and I know that hundreds are being shut out and kept from making a living by foreigners. If I were to organize a company and wanted it first-class I should select Americans all the way through.' Mr. Boucicault expresses the true American sentiment, and his words should have great weight as coming from a man who is in a position to know whereof he speaks" (p. 6).

One major discrepancy is evident in Hamsun's use of this source.

Whereas he allows the remark about Americans' preference for foreigners to stand in the first Boucicault quotation—although the exclamation point is presumably his insertion—he alters a similar observation in the *America* item. According to Boucicault, the prominence of foreign entertainers is evidence of the "cadism" of American theater audiences; in Hamsun's translation this becomes, "The pushing to the forefront of English or other European actors or actresses is simply to give the American public a slap in the face." Hamsun also ignores *America*'s introductory comment on the financial success of English actors; yet actually both Boucicault and *America*, contrary to Hamsun's thesis of American insularity and self-sufficiency, indirectly attest to the popularity of Europeans, whatever the pressure of special-interest groups.

4. The Norwegian replica in Hamsun's book—omitted here—shows a playbill, with translated text, publicizing a new comedy at the Grand Opera entitled *Our Wedding Day*. Issued in the form of a check from the Bank of Happy Laughter, it promises the bearer "one laugh per minute, worth anyone one hundred dollars," if he attends the performances of Marguerite Fish, the comedienne, whose signature appears on the check.

## THE CULTURAL HARVEST

1. Writer unknown.

2. Hamsun's ellipses denote the following omissions respectively: the sculptor's name, "Mr. Johannes Gelert"; the detail "exclusive of the pedestal"; and "of that famous massacre." *America*, December 20, 1888, p. 6.

3. Although Hamsun's denunciation of the legal action that resulted from the Haymarket riot has been largely vindicated, there are some inaccuracies in his account. Six weeks after the riot in which, among others, more than sixty policemen were injured by the actual bomb explosion, eight social revolutionaries in the city were brought to trial on June 21, 1886, soon after the death of a seventh policeman. Subsequently one more died. All the defendants, including Albert Parsons, who had addressed the crowd assembled in the square on the night of the disorder, were found guilty. Seven were sentenced to death; the eighth received a fifteen-year prison term. On the day of execution, November 11, 1887, after one of the condemned had committed suicide in his cell, the governor of Illinois commuted the sentences of two others, but the remaining four, including Parsons, were hanged that evening.

4. I have been unable to find Hamsun's source.

5. The accurate identification of John H. Rauch as secretary of the Illinois State Board of Health indicates that Hamsun had access to one

of the Board's publications, but it was not the *Eleventh Annual Report* for 1888. The Board's detailed inquiry into the status of medical educa- tion in the United States and Canada was conducted throughout the 1880s and served as the basis for a schedule of minimum requirements for certification under the state's Medical Practice Act. Numerous medi- cal schools complied with these requirements, thereby contributing to broader efforts to reduce the excessive number of practitioners by raising the standards and quality of medical education nationally. According to the *Tenth Annual Report* (1887), following enforcement of an initial schedule enacted during the 1883–1884 session, 114 medical colleges of the 129 in existence now had lecture terms of five months or over; 43 colleges also required attendance in three or more courses of lectures, and 57 others had made provision for a three- or four-year graded course. In 1891, Illinois increased its minimum requirement for professional studies to four years.

The general tenor of the quotation attributed to *America* suggests that it derives from the same source as Hamsun's other information. It does not occur in the December 20, 1888, issue, which is otherwise the ex- clusive reference in the study.

6. De Robigne Mortimer Bennett (1818–1882) was variously a quack, druggist, freethinking popularizer, and editor of the *Truthseeker*, whose irreverent treatment of religion and the clergy led in 1879 to a conviction for sending indecent matter through the mails. He was sentenced to thirteen months in prison.

7. I have been unable to find any record of this man.

8. Some of these comparisons between English and American social practices are tacitly indebted to "A Visit to Philistia," *Fortnightly Review*, n.s. XXV (January 1884), 50–64, by the English social critic Lepel Griffin. Visiting the United States in the wake of Matthew Arnold, Cole- ridge, and Henry Irving, Griffin—like Hamsun—deplored the country's materialism, the failure of its democratic institutions, its mean and sordid life. But unlike Hamsun, he also decried "the depreciatory attitude to all things English that is taken by the vast majority of Americans," espe- cially their irritating habit of extolling "every American usage or institu- tion . . . not only as good in itself, but as better than anything to be found in 'the old country'" (p. 53). Akin to this was the pronounced unpopularity of the English, although Griffin acknowledged some im- provement in recent years: "This is most evident in the eastern towns, such as Boston and New York, where the imitation of English manners and amusements has become for the time the fashion. Horse-racing has grown to large proportions, fox-hunting, lawn-tennis, and cricket are making slow progress, and the New York dude might almost compare,

for fatuous imbecility, with the London masher. So far and low have English fashions penetrated, that Mr. Stokes, the affable proprietor of the Hoffman House, keeps no waiters in his employ who will not consent to shave their moustaches and cut their whiskers *à l'Anglaise*. But in the Central and Western States, with the exception of Colorado, which is being largely developed by English settlers and capital, there is little love for England or English ways, and criticism is almost uniformly unfriendly" (p. 54). Hamsun's comparisons are necessarily secondhand, since with the exception of his brief train passage from Hull to Liverpool en route to America in 1882, he had never visited England.

9. The reference is to Bjørnson's lecture on sexual morality, "Monogamy and Polygamy," first delivered on November 13, 1887, in which he asserted that one of the basic causes of the American Civil War was opposition to the polygamous practices in the Southern states that resulted from the demoralizing institution of slavery.

## CONCLUSION

1. The three quotations are from Lepel Griffin's "A Visit to Philistia," *Fortnightly Review*, n.s. XXV (January 1884), 50, 50, 52. The bracketed ellipses in the second quote signal the omission of, first, "where political life, which should be the breath of the nostrils of every freeman, is shunned by an honest man as the plague" and, second, "and where wealth has become a curse instead of a blessing." The third quotation omits "with the single exception of Russia."

Polemical inflation and personal embellishment or adaptation notwithstanding, this development clearly evidences the use of other unacknowledged details and illustrations from the article. Griffin, for example, had pointed out the similarity between the English and Americans in their "love of big things," even though the trait was grotesquely caricatured in the latter because it was united with an equal tendency to establish money as "the standard of beauty and virtue." "At present," he noted, with Hamsun echoing him, "Americans are satisfied with things because they are large; and if not large they must have cost a great deal of money." The comment sprang in part from personal experience: "One evening, at the Madison Square Theatre, an American observed to me, 'That is the most expensive drop-scene in the world.' It was a glorified curtain of embroidery, with a golden crane and a fairy landscape, and might justly have been claimed as the most beautiful drop-scene in the world; but this was not the primary idea in the Yankee mind. The two houses most beautiful architecturally in the Michigan Avenue at Chicago were shown to me as half-a-million-dollar houses" (p. 56).

Two other illustrations that reappear in Hamsun's presentation involve

the Washington Monument, then under construction, and the Metropolitan Opera House in New York. According to Griffin, the column
was intended to reach six hundred feet, " 'the highest structure ever raised
by man, excepting the Tower of Babel.' " This was also its sole distinction. The Metropolitan Opera House, in turn, offered the most recent
demonstration of the Americans' predilection for big things. Financed by
wealthy but unmusical New Yorkers, such as Vanderbilt and Jay Gould,
the house could not compare "with those of Paris, Vienna, Moscow, and
London, which have all and each their special charm. Its architect visited
Europe, and carefully collected for reproduction everything that he could
find ugly or inconvenient, and then built the largest, the meanest, the
most ill-arranged opera-house, the worst for sight and sound, to be
found in the world" (pp. 56–57).

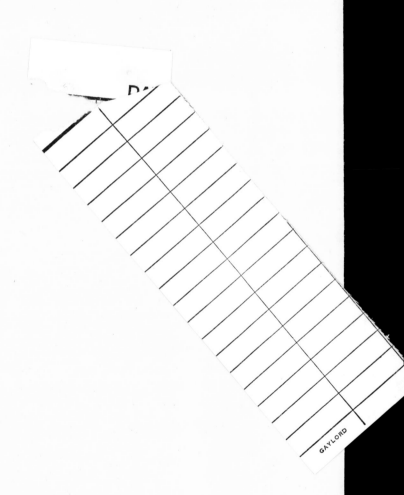